AN INTRODUCTION TO
THE USE OF
THE PUBLIC RECORDS

AN INTRODUCTION TO
THE USE OF
THE PUBLIC RECORDS

By

V. H. GALBRAITH

REGIUS PROFESSOR OF MODERN HISTORY IN THE UNIVERSITY OF OXFORD
AND FORMERLY AN ASSISTANT KEEPER OF
THE PUBLIC RECORDS

OXFORD UNIVERSITY PRESS

Oxford University Press

OXFORD LONDON NEW YORK

GLASGOW TORONTO MELBOURNE WELLINGTON

CAPE TOWN IBADAN NAIROBI DAR ES SALAAM LUSAKA ADDIS ABABA

DELHI BOMBAY CALCUTTA MADRAS KARACHI LAHORE DACCA

KUALA LUMPUR SINGAPORE HONG KONG TOKYO

FIRST PUBLISHED 1934

REPRINTED LITHOGRAPHICALLY IN GREAT BRITAIN

BY LOWE & BRYDONE (PRINTERS) LTD., LONDON, FROM SHEETS

OF FIRST EDITION 1934 (WITH CORRECTIONS), 1952 (WITH CORRECTIONS), 1963, 1971

PREFACE

THIS book is the substance of five lectures which I have given for several years in the Michaelmas Term to graduate students beginning original research. My aim has been to give a simple description of the chief classes of records and of the inter-relationship of the various branches of the administration; and at the same time to make the book as short as possible. I would like to thank the Deputy Keeper, Mr. A. E. Stamp, who read the manuscript, for some valuable suggestions; and Mr. Charles Johnson for reading the proofs. To Mr. J. R. Crompton, who also read the proofs, I am specially indebted in the last chapter; while Professor C. H. Williams has very kindly helped me with the short section on the legal records. To my wife I am grateful for help at every stage.

V. H. G.

OXFORD
September 1934

CONTENTS

I

INTRODUCTORY

THE Public Record Office stands on the east side of Chancery Lane, about 150 yards north of Fleet Street. Here in a single building are concentrated three-quarters—perhaps—of the national archives, the growing bulk of which has made it necessary to find 'overflow' depositories, at Hayes and Ashridge. Besides the records themselves and the staff to look after them, there are reading-rooms for the public and a museum which is less well known than it ought to be. For, as museums go, it is very small; and its peculiar interest lies in the fact that the exhibits have not been collected, but are all, from Domesday Book to the Scrap of Paper, public records deposited in the ordinary routine of administration. Though the whole building, archive and museum, is modern, the site has belonged for more than 500 years to the Master of the Rolls, who is the national 'keeper' of the Public Records. It is a normal government office, a part of the Civil Service, and controlled by the Treasury. The Public Record Office and the Master of the Rolls.

This arrangement goes back no farther than the nineteenth century. Prior to 1838, when the Public Record Office was founded, there was no national keeper of all the public records. Roughly speaking, there were as many keepers as there were courts or departments, and there were as many record offices Foundation of the Public Record Office, 1838.

as there were keepers. Indeed, this country has in the past century built up the most concentrated and centralized archive system in the world. It is an English peculiarity, the merits and demerits of which may be argued; but which at any rate provides an unrivalled opportunity for the serious historian. Compare, or rather contrast it with the ecclesiastical records which (even if we exclude the parish records) are divided among more than a score of cathedral chapters and as many bishops' registries: or with the arrangements of so small a country as Belgium which, in addition to the central depository at Brussels, has no less than eight local archives.

The Master of the Rolls, though to-day we think of him as a judge, was not always a legal official. The very name betrays his original duties. He began as a clerk of the Chancellor when the Chancellor was the 'secretary of State for all departments', the medieval prime minister in fact. The Chancellor himself at a still earlier period had a similar modest origin as the king's chaplain who, in the intervals of his proper duties, performed the more occasional service of writing the king's letters. He then became the keeper of the Seal, later called the Great Seal to distinguish it from other and smaller seals; and this, though he would perhaps be surprised to hear it, is still his essential function. The Chancellor was of course a *clericus*, an ecclesiastic and an intimate member of the King's Household. Gradually his secretarial functions increased until he became the head of a great department. The evolution—which is common to all western Europe—is specially marked in England by the year 1199, when the Chancellor began the practice of enrolment, that is of keeping on parchment rolls copies of the more important letters he dispatched. It was now only a question of time until he required a special clerk to keep these records, the *custos rotulorum*. Together with his eleven other colleagues of the 'first bench' the *custos rotulorum* ran the Chancery department. Soon the Chancery lost all connexion with the Household; and, ceasing to itinerate with the Court, acquired a site for the records in what thus became Chancery Lane, the site on which the Public Record Office stands to-day. With this rise in the world came the slightly grander title of Master of the Rolls, or, with his eleven colleagues, the twelve Masters in Chancery. As for the site we can trace back its history to the year 1232, when Henry III founded a *domus conversorum*, or home for converted Jews, in the road which the Templars had made from their old home in Holborn to the 'New Temple'. After the expulsion of the Jews in 1290 the institution, never very flourishing, became almost derelict, and was transferred to the Master of the Rolls. The story is commemorated in the new building by a statue of Henry III holding in his hand the chapel he founded.

The history of the Chancery department, so closely bound up with the origin of the Public Record Office and the Master of the Rolls, illustrates the essential   Limited scope of the Public Records.

characteristic of our medieval archives. Since all national administration begins in the royal Household, the public records are concerned only with the king's business. For centuries this term has a restricted and almost personal meaning. In so far as a man could keep clear of the king, his history escapes the records. A relatively small, though important, class will be found receiving privileges (for money), or as litigants (also for money); but the great majority of the population, the unfree, will go unrecorded, and, except for taxation, the bulk of freemen. Generally speaking 'the man in the street' will only come into the records as debtor, juror, or as criminal. Thus the public records—a mine of information of ever-increasing richness as the state increases its functions—are nevertheless extremely limited in their scope throughout the Middle Ages. The warning is only less necessary in the sixteenth, seventeenth, and eighteenth centuries, until, in fact, the revolutionary development of state activities which accompanied the democratic development of the nineteenth century.

Accidental character of the present arrangement. Secondly, the history of the Chancery shows that the modern archive system is no logical, unbroken development of the medieval, but something of an historical accident. In origin the Master of the Rolls is no more than the record keeper of a department. The royal and central, if hardly the national, record office of the Middle Ages was the King's Treasury and the King's Wardrobe. The royal Treasuries were in Westminster and in the Tower, strong or sacred places, which gave security. The care of the Treasury was in the hands of the Chamberlains, who were not primarily archivists but custodians of the king's money, jewels, books, and any other valuables. In course of time they developed naturally into the keepers of the Exchequer records. Then, until the Reformation, the bulk of the records, especially the legal records, were dumped in a rather casual way in the Treasuries of the Tower and Westminster, nearly all in fact except the Chancery records. The arrangement of 1838, by which the great deposits at Westminster were added to the Chancery records at the Rolls House, was merely one of convenience. Logic and history were on the side of the opposite course.

It may be argued that it did not matter whether the Chancery records were added to the Treasury records or vice versa. It is, however, important to grasp the results of the too sudden concentration of huge masses of documents not only from Westminster but from all the smaller depositories in London, not to speak of the subsequent transfers of the records of the Palatinates of Lancaster and Durham, and the Welsh records. For the sudden change in 1838 from the dispersed to the modern unitary arrangements has left ineffaceable scars on the superficially neat system of to-day. Huge quantities of records, often unsorted, uncatalogued, and even unlabelled, were brought to Chancery Lane. The inevitable result was a certain amount of confusion in which the provenance of some of this material was lost. Heroic if premature efforts

Effects of the transition to the modern system.

to make the more important parts of it available for the student led to the formation of new artificial classes, such as *Royal Letters* and *Ancient Petitions*, and the mistaken arrangements of earlier archivists were perpetuated and even made worse. The moral is plain. No prudent person can afford, in his researches, to neglect the history of the archive group with which he is dealing. Two examples, one from the medieval records, the other from the more modern colonial records, will show the value of this precaution. To this day the *Cartae Antiquae*, indubitable products of the Exchequer, are classed, to the confusion of the researcher, with the Chancery records. The mistake goes right back to the reign of Edward II, when Bishop Stapeldon carried out a thorough overhauling of the records in the Treasury at Westminster. He had them all carried to the Tower where they were catalogued and arranged. By accident the *Cartae Antiquae*, with a few other records, were not returned to Westminster. Then in the fifteenth century the Tower was handed over to the Chancery as a record office as there was no more room in Chancery Lane. In course of time the *Cartae Antiquae* thus became absorbed into the general mass of Chancery records and were very naturally classed as such when the Tower records were brought to Chancery Lane.

A second, and modern example, is the Colonial Entry Books whose history has been disentangled by Mr. Higham. In this instance two great collections of Colonial Papers, the *America and West Indies* series

The Cartae Antiquae.

The Colonial Papers.

(the papers of the Secretaries of State) and the *Board of Trade* papers were merged (up to 1688) to form a series called *Colonial Papers* with the corresponding *Entry Books*.[1] The purpose of this arrangement was to facilitate the compilation of the official *Colonial Calendar*; but soon after this passed the year 1688, it was decided to abandon the division for the more logical plan of geographical 'distribution' which, in Mr. Higham's words 'finally destroyed all historical unity of arrangement'. The confusion, it may be added, was the greater, since the year 1688, chosen as the *terminus ad quem* of the first rearrangement, was a purely accidental one, while a great many volumes which had been bound by previous offices were broken up to be thus rearranged. The net result of the changes, though they have resulted in a good and simple system, has been to increase the difficulties of the student who wishes to make a thorough investigation of the period, for he is left with the preliminary task of restoring the original *fonds*.

A certain acquaintance with the history of the public records is, in fact, an indispensable preliminary to the study of the official *Guide to the Public Records*, the real starting-point of the researcher. He will learn from it not to attach undue weight to the classification of the records, not to regard any single class of records as necessarily a complete collection of the documents it purports to bring together, not to think of the various

History of Giuseppi's Guide.

[1] *The Colonial Entry Books*, by C. S. S. Higham (S.P.C.K.), Helps for Students of History.

classes of records as water-tight divisions, and above
all he will acquire an understanding of the quite overwhelming difficulties with which the last three generations of archivists in the record office have been faced.
An elderly keeper of the records, grown rather cynical,
once remarked that it was a rooted conviction in the
minds of the public that 'the public records arrived
at Chancery Lane perfectly catalogued and arranged,
where the staff proceeded to reduce them to a state
of pie'. It was not altogether a joke: a great deal of
the evidence given before the Record Commission of
1911–14 is vitiated by ignorance of the real problem
the office has to meet.

A concrete example is supplied by the history of the
official *Guide* itself, the latest edition of which was
made by Mr. Giuseppi.[1] The work—a model of
lucidity and conciseness to-day—has been painfully
evolved from the original *Hand Book to the Public Records* by F. S. Thomas (1853). Little progress had been
made with sorting the huge collections at the then
new P. R. O. In his Handbook, therefore, he arranged
the records, as he said, alphabetically and analytically
under their various courts and departments.

'Thus should any person desire to know what surveys are among the Public Records, he will look for
the head SURVEYS: for instance, refer to the Chancery
at page 89, it is there shown what kinds of surveys are
among the Chancery Records. Again, refer to the
Exchequer. It will be there seen'—and so on. It is

---

[1] This is now out of print. A new *Guide* is planned, of which the
introductory section has appeared.

in fact a subject index. The system was carried to its logical conclusion in 1891, when a new edition of the guide was prepared by S. R. Scargill-Bird. Its object was 'to enable [the reader] to decide at a glance which and how many of the various classes will be of service to him'. Here, for example, are six consecutive entries taken at random: Genealogy—Gentleman Pensioners —Grammar Schools—Guilds and Fraternities—Accounts—Hundred Rolls. In addition to these subject indexes they made artificial classes from documents 'of similar nature, grouped together from similar sources'. So arose Rentals and Surveys, Ancient Correspondence or Royal and Historical Letters, and Ancient Petitions, mentioned above.

The steps by which this arrangement of the records has been abandoned may be traced in the *Guide*. The first doubts will be found in the second edition of Scargill-Bird; while the third is the work of a mind altogether at sea.

Turn to *Giuseppi* and you will see that it is different. The book—almost delusive in its simplicity—may be analysed as follows:

Vol. i. Records of the Chancery	. .	pp. 1–70
„ „ Exchequer	. .	pp. 71–218
Legal records . . .	.	pp. 219–95
Palatinate records . .		pp. 296–338
Special Collections . .	.	pp. 339–54

Each of these main divisions is subdivided in alphabetical order according to the names of the sub-offices or administrations which produced them: the

Exchequer into the records of the King's Remembrancer, the Lord Treasurer's Remembrancer, the Augmentation Office, and so on; the legal records into those of the King's Bench, the Common Pleas, &c.; the Chancery embracing a part of the records of the King's Council and those of Parliament as well as its own. The only exception is the Special Collections, the *damnosa hereditas* of the past whereby thousands of documents were torn from their fellows, impairing their own separate value, and the collective value of the live series to which they belonged.

A new conception of history lies behind these changes—that, in Professor Tout's words, of seeking in the past what was important to them, rather than to ourselves. To achieve our end we must put ourselves back in their times; to do this we must recreate their world, and a part of their world was their administrative system. The public records are like a skeleton, and from the dry bones we have to arrive at some conception of the living past: to see it as it was.

Modern conception of Archives. On this principle the public records cease to be a number of discrete or arbitrary subject groupings, and they become, it has been said, 'the secretions of an organism'.

The principle has been formulated by archivists as that of *respect des fonds*, the maintenance of the original administrative groupings. To maintain them, it is necessary to understand them, so that some grasp of the administrative machine is necessary before one can even begin to research on any period. This is the true line of approach to *Giuseppi's Guide* for the student of social or economic history no less than for the student of politics and institutions. It is often forgotten that the archivist has had to do his work in a world whose fundamental conceptions of what history is have been revolutionized, and the work he does is more permanent than the ideas on which it was based. The faults that now seem glaring were less evident a generation ago: were not perhaps faults at all. One need not work for long to discover that the *Guide* shares the general imperfections of all things human. By understanding one can learn how they came about and so to remedy them—however slightly—in the particular classes with which one works. The weapons will be two—a knowledge of the history of the public records and a knowledge of the workings of the various administrations of the period.

A moment's thought will show the importance to the historian of a knowledge of administrative machinery. We owe the preservation of the archives of the past to the men who staffed the Chancery, the Exchequer, and the other departments. The motive therefore for the preservation of these archives was thus originally a purely practical one. They were dead papers put by for future reference. In complete contrast with the literary sources of the past, they owe their preservation as a rule to administrative convenience alone, not to any appreciation of their historical value. They have been described as the deposit

The Formation of Archives.

left by the stream of time; but they are something more than this, for an intelligible if limited motive has controlled their selection. We shall therefore make best use of them if we approach them with the same intimate knowledge of their inter-relationship as the clerks who made and kept them. To think of them as the secretions of an organism is peculiarly appropriate in the case of the English archives. For the English Government refuses to add artificially to this deposit by the purchase[1] of records, as is the continental practice. In this way their organic unity and structure is preserved. The principle is unimpeachable, though English practice is based neither on principle nor even on parsimony; it springs rather from the attitude of the Law Courts which give to The doc-public records which have never been out of custody trine of a weight as evidence denied to other documents, Custody. which are not 'of record' and have to be 'proved' by the testimony of experts. This legal doctrine, in common with others, has not much historical basis in fact. For centuries the national archives were mainly left to rot in damp cellars or attics, in 'safe custody' in no other sense than that they were regarded as useless lumber; and while this has worked beneficially in preventing our archives from acquiring the qualities of a museum, it is partly responsible for the enormous gaps, especially among the post-Reformation departmental records. As we shall see later, large quantities

---

[1] 'Gifts and Deposits' are accepted in certain cases, but kept separate from the main body of the records.

of public records were retained by Secretaries of State, military governors, and so on, which have come in some cases into the possession of the British Museum or other libraries and in some cases remain in private hands. Overborne by the lawyer, we have not shown our boasted common sense in this matter. Beyond all question it is the duty of the State to acquire by purchase or otherwise such collections. Many have left us already for America, and many more will follow them.

In addition to the gaps in the public records there should be mentioned the real weakness in our centralized archive system. The absence, until lately, of any provincial or county record offices has cost us very dear in the matter of local records whether public or private. There was indeed a proposal in 1547 to establish county depositories, but the House of Lords threw it out. The result of this has been the loss of virtually the whole of our early county court records. This is to be deplored, it cannot be cured; but the absence of local offices is *still* costing us dear. Such depositories would serve as magnets to attract local records of all kinds, whether as gifts or on deposit. The situation has become acute since the Law of Property Amendment Act (1924) which abolished prospectively copyhold tenure. By this Act *Court Rolls*, formerly the title deeds of all copyhold land, have become so much scrap paper. Fortunately the Act, foreseeing the danger, has conferred on the Master of the Rolls power to secure a proper custody of such documents. *Need for new Depositories.*

Custody of Court Rolls.

This addition to the power of the Master of the Rolls is a most hopeful development. The Master of the Rolls is now in some sort the keeper of the national records, and the same care which has been given to the public records is now under his vigorous leadership being given to private records. A committee has been established at the Public Record Office to collect information, and a huge index of Court Rolls still surviving is being constructed. In each county at least one institution has been approved by the Master of the Rolls as a place of safe custody not only for Court Rolls but records of all kinds.[1] Thus we are beginning to acquire, however late, the nucleus of a system of local archives. It is every one's duty to guide any records he may hear of towards their proper home in these depositories. With a system of local archives co-ordinated to the splendid collections of the Public Record Office the history of England could be written with a fullness possible in no other country.[2]

[1] More recently the Master of the Rolls has been given statutory authority to provide for the preservation of Tithe Records.

[2] Since the above was written the British Records Association has given vigorous publicity to the need to preserve private and local records and been responsible for the placing of many valuable documents in safe custody. In 1945 the Hist. MSS. Commission began the compilation of a National Register of Archives, and a project for the statutory establishment of local record offices, for the custody of local, ecclesiastical and private records is being considered by a committee set up by the Master of the Rolls.

II

THE SECRETARIAT IN THE MIDDLE AGES: THE RECORDS OF THE CHANCERY, THE PRIVY SEAL, AND THE SIGNET

THE functions of the medieval central government were, broadly speaking, threefold—secretarial, financial, judicial. Of these the second and third are merely supplementary to the first, which regulates policy and is at all times most closely connected with the sovereign. It was in fact the mainspring of the whole machine, and an almost philosophic interest attaches to the primary diplomatic form in which, through their chanceries, the earliest European governments transacted their business. Since the time of the Roman Empire the essential form, borrowed from Rome, has been that of the letter, a document that is, with an address, a greeting, and a farewell. The Papal Chancery was naturally the first to take over this form, and has continued to use it with little change to this day. The new secular chanceries, like the Merovingian, perhaps followed the Papal Chancery. But in the early Middle Ages there was a tendency towards a more elaborate and impressive, not to say cumbersome form, which in the Papal Chancery was called a privilege and which, when it emanates from the lay chanceries, *we* call a diploma. These documents are remarkable for their size, and for their *Importance of the Chancery.*

The Diploma.

calligraphy. They commonly began with an invocation of the Deity, followed by a pious preamble: a clause threatening the pains of hell on those who infringed the grant; and long lists of signatories, each making the sign of the cross.

The oldest 'public records' of England are these charters of her early kings. The most ancient that survive belong to the seventh century. With the passing of the centuries the numbers grow steadily larger: for the period before the Norman Conquest the total is more than a thousand. The purpose of these charters was in nearly all cases the same—to put on record the grants of lands and privileges to noblemen and (more often) to the Church. Their form, which was stereotyped, may be illustrated by the Charter of Æthelstan to Exeter in the year 937.[1]

+ In the name of Christ! And considering with sagacious foresight the errors and failings of the human condition, of which Ecclesiastes 'Vanity of vanities', saith he, 'and all is vanity', and therefore let eternal joys be bought with perishable things, with truth saying 'Lay yourselves up treasure in Heaven, &c.'. Therefore, I, Æthelstan by God's permission king, Monarch of all the islands of Britain, freely grant a certain parcel of land, that is a manse, which the unlearned called Toppesham, to the monastery of the Church of St. Peter Apostle at Exeter, for the cure of my soul, to have in eternal freedom as long as the Christian Faith may endure. Henceforth this land is to remain free from all royal taxes, except

[1] *Ordnance Survey Facsimiles*, I. xiv, from which the translation is taken.

the common labour which is known to all. If any one henceforth take away this our grant, let him know that he is going to go against God, and not me, because from him I have received power. The bounds moreover of this land are these, first from Toppesor up along the Exe . . . [*the boundaries are set out in detail*] . . . along the stream again to Toppesor.

This grant was made in the year of the Incarnation of our Lord 937.

+ I, Æthelstan, King of all Britain have confirmed this
    grant with the Sign of the Holy Cross.
+ I, Eadmund Ætheling have consented. + I, Howel,
    Regulus. + Æthelwold, Thane.
+ I, Wulfhelm have consented. + I, Wulgar, *Dux*.
    + Ælfric, Thane.
+ I, Ælfheah have acquiesced. + Ælfhere, *Dux*.
    + Wulfsige, Thane.
+ I, Æthelgar have concluded. + Æthelstan, *Dux*.
    + Odda, Thane.

It is a very elaborate and a very ecclesiastical document, whose *formulae* took shape in a society for whom the written record was something solemn, unusual, exceptional. Between the English and continental diplomas there is a general similarity; but there is also this fundamental difference, that the former have no mark of authenticity. In France and Germany, for example, such documents bore a large wax seal impressed upon the face of the document; in England they are unsealed. Again, the foreign examples are written in a distinctive, official, cursive writing, while in England they are written in the ordinary monastic book hand. Moreover, instead of the long list of attesting witnesses which completes an English charter, foreign diplomas commonly bear the subscription of a *referendarius*, chancellor, or other officer responsible for the issue of the document. The English diplomas are indeed calligraphic rather than diplomatic documents: the multiplication of 'exemplars' or even the forgery of them was possible wherever there were trained scribes. We can in fact never say of any English 'original': 'this is the very document issued by such a king in such a year'. Diplomatically speaking, it is a very primitive type.

The sealed writ. But from the tenth century at latest the English kings were also using freely a totally different kind of document—a simple, sealed writ or letter addressed to the shire court. The first surviving example of these sealed writs belongs to the reign of Edward the Confessor, and it bears a two-faced, pendent, wax seal, the idea of which was perhaps suggested by the little leaden coin seal or *bulla* used by the Papal Chancery since the sixth century on simple letters and diplomas (or 'privileges') alike. This English seal was thus the earliest 'great seal' in the west: the idea was taken up in France by the end of the eleventh century, and the practice of sealing diplomas *en placard* abandoned.

Even more striking than the seal, was the little writ to which it was attached. Here is a specimen from the reign of Edward the Confessor.[1]

---

[1] *Ordnance Survey Facsimiles*, II, Westminster 11 (1053–66).

+ Eadward king greets Leofwine bishop and Eadwine earl and all my thanes in Staffordshire friendly: and I tell you that I have given to Christ and St. Peter at Westminster the land at Pertune and all of the things that there into belong, in wood and fields, with sac and with socne, as full and as free as it stood to myself in hand, in all things, to feed the abbot and the brother-hood that dwell within the minster: and I will not per-mit any men to oust any of the things that there into belong. God preserve you all.

Diplomatically, this is a highly developed document in two ways. It is first, very short and very simple— a complete contrast to the elaborate English diploma, and indeed to all extant documents of the period, English or foreign. Secondly, it is written in the vernacular, many generations before any other coun-try is known to have abandoned Latin. It is clearly the product of a long-established as well as a highly organized Chancery: a Chancery with a tradition behind it in a country which had already travelled far towards national consciousness.

This little writ is the *fons et origo* of later English diplomatic forms—of Charters, Letters Patent, and Letters Close. To draft, engross, seal, and dispatch these writs was the business of the Chancellor, the keeper of the king's seal. William the Bastard, who had neither seal nor chancery of his own, took over the system unchanged, substituting Latin for English. In this way the little writ came in contact with the diplomatic usage of France and so to exercise a general simplifying influence on western letter forms.

Triumph of the writ.

It was itself in turn exposed to new influences, and so in the next century developed in an intelligible if complex way into the various familiar forms of our medieval archives. The writ or something like it became the vehicle for the intercourse of civilized governments. Slowly but surely it 'killed' the diploma, with its chrisms, crosses, and curses.

This is a digression, for our Chancery archives only begin in the first year of King John. But it is not *The* without value to grasp that the English Chancery *Chancery Enrol-* was already an ancient and sophisticated institution *ments* when a close knowledge of its workings first becomes *(Out-letters).* possible. In the twelfth century it became necessary to make duplicate copies of many of these writs, called *contra brevia*, which were kept on files. At last, in the first year of King John, by a change which was in effect a revolution, the occasional procedure of making *contra brevia* was superseded by the making of systematic copies of all out-letters of importance. In England these copies were made on parchment membranes (about 12 in. × 24 in.) sewn end to end and rolled up, some thirty to each roll. The English method called enrolment (*irrotulamentum*) differed from that of the Popes and the French, who preferred the system of books or registers. We do not know for certain to whom we owe the idea, but Dr. Poole has shown good reason for thinking it was Hubert Walter. By what is probably no mere coincidence, the French registers begin at almost the same moment as the English enrolments and the Papal registers which, while they go back in some form or other to the fourth century, have only been systematically kept since 1198, the first year of Innocent III's pontificate.

The practice of enrolment marks the beginning of the archives of the English Chancery. Royal charters before 1199, both diplomas and writs, have survived only in cathedral and monastic archives, in copies made in the Exchequer, or in late exemplifications issued by the Chancery. But from 1199 till to-day the Chancery enrolments have been made and preserved in exactly the same way; and they form a most important source of English history. Beginning as a single undifferentiated annual roll for many kinds of documents the system rapidly developed until there were three main series—the rolls of Charters, or grants of lands or privileges to churches, or cities, or to a man and his heirs (*perpetuities*); rolls of Letters Patent, or documents of less dignity though also issued open (i.e. with the seal pendent from the document); and rolls of Letters Close or documents closed by the seal.[1] The last of these corresponds closely to the modern 'letter', and could only be opened by the recipient when the seal was broken. They were the routine orders of the central government to local officials, of no lasting value. The third class is of course very many times larger than the first two, letters being issued 'close' as much for con-

Marginal note: Charter, Patent, and Close Rolls.

[1] There is a Charter Roll for 1 John; the Patent Rolls begin 3 John, and the Close Rolls (according to the List of Chancery Rolls) in 6 John. Actually the Close Rolls (which grew out of the Liberate Rolls, beginning in 2 John) start a little earlier.

venience of dispatch and for economizing wax—for they did not bear the full seal—as for privacy. Letters Patent covered the wide province that lay between these purely momentary documents and the 'solemn' charters—the lineal descendant of the earlier 'diplomas'. They included grants for life, commissions, licences to alienate land, &c. These were the main classes of Chancery enrolments, but many other series and partial series grew up. The chief of these was the Fine Rolls which dealt with the sums of money promised to the king in return for grants of land.

Fine and Liberate Rolls. There were also the Liberate Rolls on which were entered the warrants sent under the Great Seal to the Exchequer to authorize the payment of money. Besides these there later appeared rolls devoted to special subjects: Gascon, French, and Scotch Rolls, Staple Rolls, and so on.

Limitations of Enrolments. No other country has any series comparable to the English Chancery enrolments either in its elaborate subdivisions or in the completeness with which they have been preserved. But they have their limitations and they have their defects. They are in the first place private memoranda for the use of the Chancery clerks and the administration. The copy on the roll was made from the draft which in some cases was altered before the engrossment was made: there was no system of examination and above all there were frequent omissions, erasures, and alterations. It was possible, for example, to accuse William of Wykeham, when Chancellor, of having freely tampered with the enrolments, when in fact the frequent alterations were probably the deliberate alteration of the original scribe. Mistakes, too, were common, while still more serious are the omissions. None of these rolls is an absolutely complete record. Some classes of documents never were enrolled, and many others only if the beneficiary wished it, and paid for it. Slackness and error perhaps account for the omission of a still larger number.

The argument *a silentio* where the Chancery Rolls are concerned is nearly always worthless. It should also be mentioned that there was no system of indexing. Unless, therefore, one is lucky enough to be consulting a roll of which the Public Record Office has published a Calendar, it is necessary laboriously to unroll and examine 30 or 40 feet of parchment to look at the face of the roll and then unroll it once more to examine the *dorse*, assisted only by brief marginal headings. This difficulty was overcome to some extent by the rapid division of enrolments into the subject classes mentioned above; while at the same time in a few cases, e.g. the Patent and Close Rolls, the front (*recto*) of the roll was reserved for certain definite types of documents, the back (*dorse*) for others.

The beginner, too, should be warned that the Chancery enrolments are heavily abbreviated (I do not refer to the writing which is of course contracted) by reducing the common form at the beginning and end of the letter to a minimum. Thus in a Letter Patent of Richard II 'Ricardus dei gratia rex Anglie et Francie et dominus Hibernie omnibus ad quos presentes littere pervenerint salutem 'will be abstracted as 'R[ex] omnibus ad quos 'etc salutem': and 'in cuius rei testimonium has litteras nostras fieri fecimus patentes. Teste meipso' as 'in cuius etc. T[este] R[ege]'. The date of the letter is, of course, retained in the enrolment, though this, too, may be contracted to 'T[este] ut supra' when it is the same as that of the preceding document.

Admini- The main divisions of the Chancery enrolments
strative continued for centuries: some, like the Patent and
Develop- Close Rolls (the latter now in books), survive to this
ments day. But the administrative machine itself was changing slowly all through the Middle Ages. When enrolment began the king for the most part was still at hand to give his orders by word of mouth. In the Chancery the thirteenth century grew into a great department, with a regular office and a fixed routine. Little by little it ceased to itinerate regularly with the king and gradually acquired a permanent head-
The Privy quarters at Westminster. The king began to send
Seal. his orders to the Chancellor in writing, using for the purpose his small or Privy Seal. From the time of Edward I we find in the Chancery archives a large class of warrants under the Privy Seal authorizing the issue of letters under the Great Seal. A new household secretariat had arisen, the work of which overlapped and to some extent competed with that of the Chancery.

Still a third royal seal appears in the first half of _{The} the fourteenth century, when the Privy Seal in its ^{Signet.} turn went out of Court (in fact if not in theory), its keeper becoming with the Chancellor and Treasurer one of the three great officers of State, who together formed a *quorum* and so could act as the King's Council. The result was the evolution of a third secretariat—the Signet Office, with its keeper the King's Secretary. The same developments took place *pari passu* in France, with this difference, that France while multiplying its seals retained the Chancery as a single all-embracing secretariat. The new seals were not departmentalized.

These consecutive developments greatly compli- Growing cated the issue of documents. If we choose a moment, complexity of Chan- say in the reign of Henry IV, we shall find it is now cery quite exceptional for the king to tell his Chancellor process. by word of mouth to dispatch a document. The normal procedure has grown much more intricate. Suppose a town or an abbey wants a grant of new privileges or the confirmation of old ones. A petition is first presented to the king. If it is granted the King's Secretary will send a warrant sealed with the Signet to the Keeper of the Privy Seal instructing him in turn to send the Chancellor under the Privy Seal a warrant for the issue of the privileges so granted or confirmed. The warrant under the Signet is filed in the Privy Seal office, that under the Privy Seal in the Chancery, which will draft the necessary letters, enrol them on the appropriate roll, engross and seal as many copies (*exemplaria*) as the beneficiary requires, and finally when all fees have been paid, issue them to him from the Hanaper department of the Chancery.

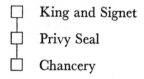

By the end of the fourteenth century this is the normal process for the issue of instruments under the Great Seal. It was of course clumsy in the extreme, wasteful both in time and money, for the beneficiary had to pay fees at every stage. So cumbrous was it that the Crown always retained the right—though there was a good deal of opposition—to send *immediate* warrants to the Chancellor in writing or by the mouth of a messenger which cut out the two stages of Signet and Privy Seal.

Admini-
strative
conveni-
ence the
key to
these
develop-
ments.

The way in which these changes came about is the province of the historian of administration. But a fact of fundamental importance for the student of archives lies behind them all. It is this. To the end of the Middle Ages and indeed long after, the king, in spite of all parliamentary and political struggle, remained the active governing head of the kingdom. He not only initiated policy: he was also personally concerned in carrying it out. The growth of these new secretariats was, therefore, due in the last resort purely to administrative convenience. They were the inevitable outcome of the ever-growing responsibilities thrown upon the king and his Household—the governing centre of the kingdom. The growth of an elaborate Exchequer department, of a Chancery department, of the great courts of law, helped the king to get through the work of state in the twelfth and thirteenth centuries. The development of Privy Seal and Signet secretariats and the elaborate organization of the Council gave him the same assistance in the fourteenth century. And when all this departmentalism had taken place, the king and the King's Household remained the actual governing body. The infinite ramifications of these administrative developments in the political struggles of the time does not alter the fact that they arose from sheer administrative necessity. That they could and did in fact often act as a check on royal autocracy was only in the nature of things. In the fourteenth and early fifteenth centuries indeed these checks tended to take the place of the crude method of rebellion—usual both earlier and later—by which the barons, the king's natural advisers from start to finish, in that aristocratic world, sought to resist the inevitable process of centralization.

The overwhelming force of what I have called 'administrative convenience' will come home to any one who uses record evidence. A great deal has been made of the difference between the French and the English secretariats. In France there were many seals—the same seals as in England—but France retained the Chancery as a single comprehensive

The French and English Chanceries.

secretariat. The new seals were not, as in England, departmentalized. But that there was much if any political significance behind this difference is difficult to believe. The almost simultaneous appearance in England and France of the same seals is itself an argument against any political interpretation: and the impression is only confirmed by the study of their interaction. For the relations of the king with the Privy Seal and the Great Seal are not peculiar. Precisely similar rules govern the practice of the Council. We can go even farther and say that any officer within the sphere of his department, admirals, generals, and so on, will use these secretariats in the same way. To be complete, therefore, our diagram should read

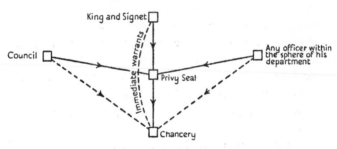

Unity of the system. Thus with all their formal differences from French practice in their workings the three English secretariats form a single, great administrative machine for the discharge of the routine of business. This essential unity by which the Great Seal was at the disposal of all other branches of the administration is reflected by the notes of warranty which the clerks added to the copies of the documents which they enrolled on the various Chancery Rolls, and which it became more and more the custom to enter on the engrossments as well. Thus an immediate warrant from the king was noted *per ipsum regem*, from the Council as *per consilium*. A warrant from the Privy Seal as *per breve de privato sigillo*: a warrant from the Treasurer as *per billam de thesaurario*, and so on. Further, it will be observed that the Privy Seal acted as a great clearing-house for all other branches of the administration—including the household—which normally transmitted their orders through the Privy Seal, though on occasion they could send them direct. Thus we can only tell in what branch of the administration an order *originated* when it did *not* follow the ordinary course but was sent direct to Chancery. The point is of real importance to students of departmental history, e.g. the Council.

Notes of warranty.

    The precise way in which this complicated system worked is very imperfectly known. We have no treatise like the Dialogue of the Exchequer to help us solve the many difficulties of Chancery practice. To three questions in particular it is hard to give a satisfactory answer. On what principle were Chancery writs dated? Why were some enrolled and others not, and why do such a large proportion of those that were enrolled bear no note of warranty? The extent of our present knowledge on the first two of these questions is accurately defined in Sir H. C. Maxwell-

Their origin.

Lyte's *Notes on the Great Seal*. On the third, fresh light
has recently been thrown by the present Deputy
Keeper of the Records. According to Mr. Stamp[1]
these notes were intended for the information of the
Chancellor at the time of sealing. He points out that
in the early thirteenth century, when the practice of
enrolment was being systematized, nearly all orders
were given by word of mouth to the *clerici de precepto*,
that is, Chancery clerks in attendance upon the king
and the Council. 'One may imagine the king sitting
regularly day by day at some definite time to transact
business, the ordinary members of the Council and
the Chancellor being present and clerks *de precepto* in
attendance. No authorization note would be required
for resulting writs. But when the king did any business
on his own account and gave instructions to the clerk
himself or allowed some official to do so, the Chancellor would need to be informed of this before sealing.'
Thus writs in general fell into two classes—writs *de
cursu* (of course) and writs *de precepto*; and of the
latter only those needed notes of warranty of which
the Chancellor had no previous knowledge at the
time of sealing. On such an explanation we may
expect to find an increasing number of such notes as
we approach the crisis of 1258, and this is exactly
what happened.

The prac-   The value of a knowledge of this process is obvious
tical value enough. It cannot be assumed that, because no
of this
compli-
cated   [1] *Some Notes on the Court and Chancery of Henry III* (Essays presented
process. to James Tait).

evidence of a particular transaction is found on the relevant Chancery Roll, no evidence survives. The document though not enrolled may be found in substance among the warrants for the Great Seal, i.e. the authorizations under the Privy Seal which the Chancery filed and on which they acted. If these fail, there is still a chance that the warrant for the Privy Seal survives, i.e. the document sealed with the Signet which was filed by the Privy Seal Office and was *their* warrant for writing to the Chancery. Thus excluding the engrossment (or the 'original' as it is loosely called) which was issued to the beneficiary there are three chances of finding a document issued under the Great Seal. As a matter of fact, the chances, as will be seen, are even greater, for a copy of the document or at least a proof that such a document was issued can often be traced in the Exchequer records and sometimes even in those of the Courts of Law. The administration in fact formed an organic whole whose branches were so closely related that none of them can be safely studied in isolation.

All this, however, though true, is only half the truth or less. For the relations of both Privy Seal and Signet with the Chancery were but an insignificant fragment of their activities. Each had besides what we may call its original jurisdiction and dispatched directly writs by the thousand on innumerable matters of routine which did not require the use of the Great Seal. Their direct activities included both the most trivial and the most important corre-

Original activity of the Privy Seal and Signet.

spondence of the government—orders to huntsmen or tradesmen and weighty and secret negotiations with the Pope or the King of France. As the Middle Ages advanced the Great Seal became increasingly formalized, and it is not too much to say that the fourteenth-century equivalent of the later *State Papers Foreign and Domestic* is to be sought in the activity of the Privy Seal Office. I say 'to be sought' advisedly, for, apart from the warrants preserved in Chancery, the Privy Seal has left us practically no archives. This gap in our materials for the history of the later Middle Ages is due to the fact that neither Signet nor Privy Seal officers kept enrolments of the documents they issued. The absence of such archives is a peculiar handicap to the historian of the fourteenth and fifteenth centuries, and explains at least to some extent why the history of this period lacks the vividness and insight into character and events which is possible both for the thirteenth and the sixteenth. But it is fortunately a loss which is not wholly irreparable. The archives of France and Spain and the Papacy will in time give us the text of many of the most important of these letters derived from the engrossments actually sealed and dispatched, while a painful search in monastic cartularies is bringing to light enough to illustrate the course of domestic history. However that may be we shall not find much of the inner history of these centuries on our Chancery Rolls. Much of it has in fact perished, a fact which is throwing us back more and more upon the literary evidence, that is, of the chronicles of the period.

The Chancery enrolments, by reason of their com- *The Chancery Files (In-letters).* pleteness the most important record source of medieval history, are but one, and that the smaller of the two great classes of Chancery documents. At the close of the Middle Ages there survived a vast and noble series of Chancery files. One small subdivision of these were the internal memoranda circulating within the various branches of the central administration, of which the Chancery Warrants, dealt with above, are a typical specimen. Infinitely larger was the other subdivision which we may call the 'in-letters', consisting of returns to writs sent out by the Chancery, inquisitions, and miscellaneous correspondence, certificates, and petitions. You can recognize a document that has been on the files by the little hole in the centre through which it was strung on the file. They should perhaps have been mentioned before the enrolments, for there must have been files for generations before enrolment was thought of. But historically their value is not now so great as that of the enrolments owing to the accidents of time by which they have become dispersed. Many of them fell apart as with the passage of time the strings broke which often held together several thousand documents. Indefatigable students like Prynne in the seventeenth century broke up, and rearranged many more, while still others, it is to be feared, suffered during the nineteenth century in the formation of the various 'Special

Collections'. The scope of the Chancery Files is thus described by Mr. C. Johnson who has spent many years in restoring their ancient *fonds*. 'Here', he says, 'were to be found the diplomatic and political correspondence of the King and his Chancellor and the drafts of many of the letters sent out, as also such of the letters or writs as were returned to the Chancery with the answers endorsed or annexed.'

The Chancery Miscellanea. In this summary description of the Chancery records there is one other class which should be mentioned—the Chancery Miscellanea. It is not, I need hardly say, an ancient division. So far as it represents anything, it represents our failure as archivists. A great deal of it is not Chancery at all. One great section is made up of the *disjecta membra* of the records of the King's Household: another of diplomatic documents—the history of our foreign policy. It is a very big class—much bigger even than the seven pages devoted to it in *Giuseppi's Guide* would suggest. Included too are a large army of waifs and strays, documents which have been separated from their fellows and have thus lost a part of their meaning. To the researcher it is thus something of a 'lucky bag' and in this connexion it is important to remember that, unlike most other records of first importance, no List of Chancery Miscellanea as a whole has yet been printed.

III

THE EXCHEQUER AND THE LEGAL
RECORDS

As with the Chancery, so with the financial depart- Origin of
ments—they spring from the royal household, the Ex-
whose earliest officers were the royal chamberlains. chequer.
A contemporary life of Edward the Confessor gives
us an apparently true picture of the king lying on his
bed while a scullion creeps into the room and steals
a handful of the king's treasure from a box under the
bed which Hugh the Chamberlain had incautiously
left open. After the Norman Conquest, financial,
like other relations, grew rapidly more complicated,
and in the course of the twelfth century a great
financial department grows up, which by Henry II's
reign was virtually separate from the Court. We know
this because it had its own seal, a duplicate (in the
strict sense) of the Great Seal. It still had the lay
chamberlains of Edward the Confessor's day, who
actually paid and received cash in what was called
the Exchequer of Receipt. But on this had now
been superimposed an accounting department, an
Exchequer of Account which was staffed by clerks.
These had become necessary with the growth of an
elaborate system of written records, the use of 'tallies'
or notched sticks, as receipts, being now restricted to
the illiterate chamberlains. It is not, therefore, sur-
prising that a new official had appeared as head of

the whole financial organization—the Treasurer, who was like the Chancellor a *clericus*. Twice a year, at Easter and Michaelmas, the sheriffs and other local officers of the Crown appeared at Westminster to answer to their debts at a special session of the king's *curia* in the Exchequer of Account.

The *Dialogus de Scaccario*. We know much more about the early growth of the Exchequer—the earliest of government departments—than of the Chancery, chiefly owing to a remarkable description of it, the Dialogue concerning the Exchequer, written in 1179 by Richard Fitz Nigel, the Treasurer. He was the grandson of Roger, Bishop of Salisbury, who seems to have been to the Exchequer what Hubert Walter was later to the Chancery. The Dialogue, for example, explains how the King's Treasury, presided over by the King's Treasurer, came to be called the Exchequer. In origin the Exchequer was no more than the chequered cloth—suggesting a chess-board, on which the reckoning was done by means of counters. It was in fact a method of arithmetic, the abacus system, which superseded the older duodecimal system in the reign of Henry I. Richard Fitz Nigel rather grimly likens the annual audit of the sheriffs to a game of chess, one side striving to increase, the other to reduce the payment due. Thus the name of Exchequer came to be commonly used of the whole organization.

The Treasury. The King's Treasury, however, remained. To the Treasurer and Chamberlains anything for preservation in the Treasury was handed over in the Court of Receipt, which soon acquired a staff of clerks, and a seal of its own, and—in time—an elaborate series of written records. It even developed—by the fifteenth century—a separate Treasury of Records, the treasury of the Receipt in Westminster Palace, distinct from the older treasuries in the Chapel of the Pyx and in the Tower of London. The confusing series of medieval treasuries of which we hear continually in the records have a closer bearing on research than might appear at first sight. For while the Chancery had evolved by the thirteenth century its own archivist, the *custos rotulorum*, and the Court of Common Pleas its *custos brevium*, neither the financial department (whether we call it Treasury or Exchequer) nor even the Crown itself possessed any special official to keep its records, until the growth of the Treasury of the Receipt. The most personal records of the Crown—its treaties, homages, Papal Bulls, and so on, were kept in special *Treasuries of the Wardrobe* in the Tower and Westminster Abbey, along with the Crown jewels, plate, books, &c. The Exchequer or Treasury had separate Treasuries, as we have seen, both in the Tower and the Abbey (Chapel of the Pyx), while a distinct treasury of records grew up at the very end of the Middle Ages in the department of the Receipt.

The Exchequer is our most perfect example of a medieval institution viewed as a growing organism. Throughout the Middle Ages it slowly developed, ever-changing and growing more complicated as the

Development of Exchequer Records.

increase of business and administrative convenience
demanded. Its importance is fundamental in our
history and a mastery of its working, say in the twelfth
century, will only lead us astray in the fourteenth,
unless we grasp the nature of the intervening development. Not unnaturally it has evolved a huge litera-
ture and still we are only on the fringe of understanding its secrets. Some of the changes—like those of
1290 or the sweeping reforms of Walter Stapeldon,
Bishop of Exeter and Treasurer in Edward II's reign
—are assignable to definite ordinance or can at least
be pinned down to a fairly definite moment. But for
the most part it is a silent, anonymous development
in response to administrative necessities and convenience, marked by the almost imperceptible transforma-
tion of one class of records or the gradual beginning
of another. Thus for the twelfth century we have,
chiefly, the Great Rolls of the Exchequer, the so-called
Pipe Rolls, the earliest of which is for 31 Henry I,
while the complete series begins with the second year
of Henry II and continues almost unbroken. With the
seventh year of Henry II we come to a fragment of a
Receipt Roll, and these become a continuous series in
the seventh year of Richard I. The Memoranda Rolls
begin in John's reign and the Issue Rolls in 5 Henry
III. All these series, according to a widespread practice of Exchequer accounting, were kept more or less
in duplicate, which gives the roll of any particular year
a double chance of survival. But it is well to remember that these double series sometimes bear different

names, and that the extent to which the one duplicates the other varies from the virtually identical
duplicate Receipt and Issue Rolls, through the closely
analogous, but still variable Pipe and Chancellors'
Rolls to the two quite separate series of Memoranda
Rolls. These were kept by two distinct departments,
that of the Lord Treasurer's and King's Remembrancer respectively, and while much is common to
both rolls, a good deal is peculiar to each. Further
and subtle developments such as the Exannual Rolls
(beginning in Edward I's reign) and the rolls of
Foreign Accounts which survive from 43 Henry III
took place in the late thirteenth and fourteenth centuries, while the fifteenth century gave rise to a more
revolutionary change—the system of Declaring Accounts before the Lord High Treasurer. Finally, we
may note the complications introduced by the Reformation which gave rise to a series of new Courts,
such as that of Augmentations and the Court of
First Fruits and Tenths.

The effect of all these changes, too complicated and
too numerous for even the most summary description,
was that the Exchequer was departmentalized in a
way that the Chancery was not. Its vast organization
is in this respect an anticipation of what was to hap-
pen to the secretariat only in the nineteenth century.
This departmentalism of the Exchequer has been
recognized in the arrangement of the records, and
hence in the *Guide* they are arranged in great *fonds*
corresponding to the following departments:

The Exchequer Departmentalized.

King's Remembrancer;

The Lord Treasurer's Remembrancer;

The Augmentation Office;

The Office of First Fruits and Tenths;

The Office of the Auditors of the Land Revenue;

The Office of the Clerk of the Pleas, all being subdivisions of the Exchequer of Accounts; and the
Exchequer of Receipt.

There is, it will be noticed, among these no *Scacca-
rium Judeorum*, or special Exchequer of the Jews, as it
has now been shown that 'the revenue from Jewish
sources passed through the regular channels of receipt and audit of the Exchequer', the special rolls
for Jewish receipts being a matter of official convenience, analogous to the French and Scotch Rolls of
the Chancery.

The
Exchequer
Year.
One characteristic, however, all Exchequer records
share in common—the peculiarity of their dating.
Both the Chancery and the Exchequer dated their
documents according to the 'years of the king', which
by the Chancery were simply calculated from the day
either of the king's accession or of his coronation.
The Exchequer year was regulated by the great
annual audit of accounts at Michaelmas with which
it ended; and the difficulty lay in harmonizing these
Exchequer years with the regnal years. As late as the
reign of Edward I the practice was to number the
Exchequer years in accordance with the regnal year
in which Michaelmas—the last day of the Exchequer
year—fell. Thus the earliest Pipe Roll which ran

from 30 September 1129 to 29 September 1130 is described as that of 31 Henry I because Henry I came to the throne in August and the 29 September 1130 fell in his thirty-first regnal year. With the death of Edward I on 7 July 1307, in his thirty-fifth regnal year, this practice was abandoned and henceforth 'a Pipe Roll bears the date of the regnal year to which the greatest part of the period of account belongs'.[1] Thus the Roll made up on 29 September 1307 was described as that of Edward I's thirty-fifth year which had begun on 16 November 1306. On the same principle there is no Pipe Roll for the twentieth year of Edward II, whose reign ended on 25 January 1327, eight months of the last period of account falling within the reign of his son. This second method of Exchequer dating lasted as late as the reign of Edward IV; and failure to grasp the change of method has given rise to a great deal of confusion in dating the records.

The Exchequer records are thus an even more imposing block than those of the Chancery. The Exchequer was already what it was ever after to be—a privileged department and its most famous series, the 'Pipe Rolls', are indeed the best written, the most costly, and generally the most impressive products of medieval administration. Instead of pieces of parchment sewed end to end in a continuous roll, the Exchequer adopted the more convenient arrangement

The Pipe Rolls.

---

[1] H. G. Richardson, 'The Exchequer Year' (*R. Hist. Soc. Transactions*, 1925), and C. R. Cheney, *Handbook of Dates*.

of a bunch of membranes fastened together at the head. Each of these was called a 'pipe' and consisted of two fine skins sewn together. The writing was a fine engrossing hand, traditional in the department, and the Pipe Roll had a formality and precision which is wanting in the more casual Chancery Rolls. This was due in part to the fact that it was written before the arrival of the sheriffs and other accountants at Westminster—spaces being left for the insertion of the actual figures; and this was possible because each roll was to a great extent a repetition of the preceding. Two of its largest sections contained the record of bad debts of many years standing (repeated year by year) and the details of fixed annual payments by the various sheriffs. The most valuable headings are, of course, those that refer to the transactions of the past year which were headed *Nova Placita* and *Nove Conventiones*, later *Nova Oblata*. These rolls beginning with 31 Henry I and virtually complete from 2 Henry II are the best record source for the twelfth century. Thanks to the Pipe Roll Society and the old Record Commission they are printed in full to the year 10 Richard I and the series is still proceeding. The conservative habits of the Exchequer (which until its last day—*dies mortis Scaccarii* in 1833, clung to the use of Roman figures) complicates the study of these records, but a few hours with Mr. Johnson's[1] introduction to the first volume of the new series will enable any one to make good use of

[1] Pipe Roll 2 Richard I (New Series, No. 1, 1925).

them. Besides the light they throw on financial and political history they are invaluable—as the late Horace Round showed us—for genealogy and for the itinerary of Henry II. The later Pipe Rolls are best approached by means of Miss Mills's[1] lucid little treatise which better than anything else illustrates their inter-relations with the records of the Chancery and the Law Courts.

In this connexion two other records are of peculiar value. The *Originalia* Rolls (L.T.R.[2]) are extracts from the Chancery Rolls by means of which the Exchequer was informed of all writs, letters, and charters on which fines were payable, which, of course, it was the sheriff's duty to collect. They thus form the link between the two departments; and are fortunately preserved from the eleventh year of Henry III. Co-operation between the two departments was further secured by the Chancery practice of making duplicates of the *Inquisitions post mortem*— or inquiries into the land held by a tenant in chief at his death, the duplicates being forwarded to the Exchequer. The corresponding links with the Law Courts are the *Estreats* or Extracts (K.R.[3] and L.T.R.). These communicated the amercements made in the Courts, which it was also the sheriffs' business to collect. The Estreats were sent to the Exchequer to provide the material for the Summonses of the Green Wax.

Co-operation of Chancery, Exchequer, and the Law Courts.

[1] The Pipe Roll for 1295: Surrey Membrane (Surrey Record Society, xxi, 1924).   [2] Lord Treasurer's Remembrancer.
[3] King's Remembrancer.

The essentially unitary character of the whole administrative system can be illustrated from still another side. The process of 'going out of Court' which determined successively the evolution of the Chancery and the Privy Seal, also governed, as we have seen, the Exchequer. Each of these 'acquired an existence separate and independent in essentials from that of the king's household'[1]—but the 'primitive un-differentiated household organization' not only con-tinued in existence, but in the thirteenth century was itself rapidly extended. Thus the Wardrobe and the Chamber, though they could not by the nature of things leave the Court, became highly developed departments with a large staff of clerks producing great quantities of records. Nor were these Household departments less concerned with public or national business than the Chancery and Exchequer. But we have no surviving *fonds* of Household records. They have disappeared, nor can we exactly explain why, and we should know little of the activities of the Household but for the fact that many of its accounts survive in the Exchequer where they were audited. There thus fortunately survive a mass of Wardrobe accounts enrolled on the Pipe Rolls and later on special Rolls called the Foreign Rolls. The Issue Rolls are also of great importance for Household operations, since they contain the substance of the 'warrants for issue' of money to royal creditors. There are finally a good many of the original detailed Ward-

[1] Tout, *Chapters*, i. 19.

robe accounts, generally in the form of books, which were presented to the Exchequer for audit, and of which a more summary copy was entered on the Roll of Foreign Accounts. The rest of what we know of the Household departments is largely drawn from the Chancery enrolments, especially from the early Close Rolls which contain orders under the Great Seal to Wardrobe officials, no less than to those of the Exchequer or the Courts of Law. The interdependence of Chancery, Household, and Exchequer was thus so close that it has been possible for Professor Tout to write the lost history of the one from the archives of the other two departments.

The third branch of medieval administration can be dealt with even more summarily. Justice, no less than the Chancery and the financial organization, springs from the King's Household, which has its *justiciarii* who in early times helped the still undifferentiated *Curia Regis* to decide legal questions. They soon evolved a procedure superior to that of the local courts of shire and hundred or, indeed, of the honorial courts of the barons, whose legal competence was steadily reduced by the system of *justiciarii itinerantes*. The itinerant justices visited the local courts and developed the system of royal writs by which cases could be transferred to the King's Court. Thus grew slowly the centralized system of justice, which crystallized out in the two great Courts of King's Bench and Common Pleas. Both these tribunals 'went out of Court' in exactly the same way as the Chancery and the

The Growth of the Common Law Courts.

Exchequer. They became departments for routine judicial business, while the King's Court continued to deal with matters of the highest importance in the King's Council. This development took place in the thirteenth century and it had tremendous results. For the Common Law Courts, as they came to be called, slowly developed a tradition of legal independence which was fostered both by their comparative ignorance of Roman Law and by the gradual growth of the Inns of Court, from which they were recruited. The apprentices of the Inns of Court were laymen to be sharply distinguished from the *clerici* who alone could enter a university, and so the Common Law was gradually transformed into the first lay profession. By the fourteenth century a sharp line was being drawn between the Common Law dispensed in the Common Law Courts of King's Bench, Common Pleas, and Exchequer (for it too had developed a court) and the conciliar jurisdiction, the King's Council and its delegated jurisdiction—the Court of Chancery. The latter were deeply impregnated with the traditions of Roman Law, canon and civil, and the distinction between the two was most clearly seen in the summary, efficient written procedure of the one set of courts, and the system of spoken argument, interminable appearances, and essoins, and the invariable use of the Jury system in the other. The House of Commons was the great champion of the Common Law system from the time of Edward III to the failure of the Lancastrian system and with the decline of the Commons, rose to importance a whole system of conciliar courts—Star Chamber, Court of Requests, the Council of the North, and the Council of Wales.

The earliest stage in this long development—that The *Curia* is the actual evolution of the King's Bench and Common Pleas—can now be studied at first hand in what is in many ways the most important record publication of this generation. These are the *Curia Regis* Rolls, published by the Deputy Keeper of the Records and edited by Mr. Flower. Some of the early rolls were published by Palgrave a century ago, but Mr. Flower has collected and systematically arranged the whole of the early rolls which are published *in extenso* to the sixth year of Henry III. There is no better initiation into the more complicated and far larger Plea Rolls—not yet even calendared or likely to be—than the study of these volumes.

In one form or another the distinction between The *Curia* pleas held before the king (*Coram Rege*) and pleas of the *Regis* and Bench (*de Banco*) is as old as the reign of Henry II, but Rolls. their final separation into two distinct courts was scarcely completed before the reign of Edward I. The difficulty has been met in the exhaustive official *List of Plea Rolls* (List and Indexes, no. 4) by an undifferentiated classification as *Curia Regis* Rolls to the end of Henry III's reign, from which point two separate series of *de Banco* and *Coram Rege* Rolls begin. Of these the former contains civil pleas between subject and subject: the latter criminal actions whether brought by a subject or on the initiative of the Crown —proceedings for trespass by bill, appeals of felony, indictments, proceedings in Error, and so on. The Assize and Eyre Rolls, the Gaol Delivery Rolls, and the Coroners' Rolls are also listed in this volume, and the prudent searcher will trust no other copy than that kept in the Round Search Room which notes all the inevitable corrections, especially valuable for the study of these documents.

Compari-son of legal records with those of Chancery and Ex-chequer. In outward form as in substance the Plea Rolls present interesting points of contrast with the records of the Chancery and Exchequer. For example, they followed the Exchequer plan of fastening a bunch of membranes at the head, writing on both sides of each leaf, in contradistinction to the Chancery method of a continuous roll. The period covered by each roll was equally distinctive. For while the Chancery following the regnal year used annual rolls, and the Exchequer (Issue Rolls) knew only two terms, Easter and Michaelmas, the Pleas Rolls are divided into the four terms of the legal year, Hilary, Lent, Trinity, and Michaelmas, one roll for each term. They had too, of course, like the Chancery and Exchequer their distinctive and traditional scripts, which show very naturally, the highest development of 'currency' in medieval court hand (since the rolls were actually written in court) and are in striking contrast with the beautiful engrossing hand of the Pipe Rolls. They are in fact more rough and ready, not to say slovenly productions than either the Exchequer or Chancery

Rolls: the scripts are coarser and the parchment inferior. In the reign of Edward I they measured about 9 in. × 24 in., and a roll of ordinary size will contain as many as 300 membranes. A last point of comparison with the Exchequer may be noted—the practice of making duplicate, or largely duplicate, rolls. Just as the Exchequer has its two series of Memoranda Rolls (K.R. and L.T.R.), and its two series of Great Rolls (Pipe and Chancellor's), so the Common Pleas has its Justices' and Rex Rolls. In this case the Rex Roll is an entirely separate and smaller roll, which, it has been conjectured, was a temporary roll sent into the Exchequer, until the fuller and more authoritative Roll of the Justices was finally deposited there. The problem, however, is not an important one for the general searcher who will do well to confine his attention to the more important Justices' Roll. The name Rex Roll is differently applied in the *Coram Rege* rolls of the King's Bench. There each roll is divided into two parts, separately numbered. Each membrane of the first part bears the name of the Chief Justice in the top right-hand corner, while the membranes of the second half are each labelled Rex. In this case the distinction is important as—roughly speaking—the first part will contain actions initiated by private plaintiffs, while the Rex Roll contains cases referred by J.P.s, presentments of Juries, cases that is on which the Crown is taking action.

For the undifferentiated period the printed *Curia Regis* Rolls mentioned above make the best introduc- Printed aids to legal search.

tion, while for each of the fully developed series of Plea Rolls there is in print a specimen of the greatest value to the beginner. Vol. no. xxxiii of the *Lists and Indexes* contains a calendar of the *de Banco* Roll for the first two years of Edward III, which will bring home as nothing else can the immensity of these records. Similarly, the British Record Society has published in full the *Coram Rege* Roll for Trinity term 1297, edited by W. Phillimore. Other works very useful as specimens are the Northampton and Lincoln Assize Rolls edited by Lady Stenton: Pleas of the Crown for the County of Gloucester, edited by Maitland: Select Pleas of the Crown (Selden Society), ed. Maitland, and Mr. Bolland's *Eyre of Kent* also in the Selden Society. For the forms of the writs used one may turn to the *Registrum Omnium Brevium*.

Inter-relation-ship of legal records.

Finally, it should be noted that the legal records are perhaps more closely interrelated than those of any other court. Thus, for example, the *de Banco* Rolls must be studied in intimate relationship with the splendid series of Feet of Fines recording conveyances of land made on a fictitious action before the Justices. The *Coram Rege* Rolls are intertwined with other surviving series in ways as intimate but more intricate. Thus cases of error may be traced to the *de Banco* Rolls; some few pleas may be carried on from the Gaol Delivery Rolls; and (still more important) the *Ancient Indictments*, where they survive, will often give us a fuller account than that found in the *Coram Rege* Roll. Again, there are the (annual) Controlment Rolls which, probably kept for office purposes, serve as an index to the Rex Roll of the *Coram Rege*. Finally, the early stages of some actions will be found on the Coroners' Rolls which, however, grow steadily more incomplete as the Middle Ages advance.[1]

And then there are the Year Books, the earliest of 'vernacular reports of an oral debate', made 'by learners for learners', 'by apprentices for apprentices'. They are not archives (much less 'public archives'), but unofficial extracts of cases, beginning in the second half of Edward I's reign. They lie scattered in libraries and are gradually being printed. But with them is bound up the whole development of the Inns of Court and therefore of English Law. The connexion of the Year Books with the Plea Rolls is obvious. They provide a means of getting behind the wilderness of 'common form' which faces our search of the Plea Rolls. Verdicts are important—all important for political history, and even proceedings without a verdict often tell us much. But for the growth of law the Year Books are probably more important than the rolls. The two are in any case complementary and each makes the other more full of meaning. For such reasons the Year Books published by the Selden Society give, wherever they can be found, the substance of the relative entries from the Plea Rolls, and these volumes make an excellent introduction to the serious study of medieval law.

The Year Books.

[1] See G. O. Sayles, *Select Pleas in the Court of King's Bench under Edward I.* Vol. I (1936).

Difficulties in using the Plea Rolls. The connexion of the legal records with those of the Exchequer has been noticed above, but the interrelationship of their archives is a warning, not less weighty than that offered by the Chancery records, of the danger of research divorced from a close understanding of the whole process of administration. It is not enough to study the documents *separatim*; nor even to follow the history of the records. We must as intimately as possible grasp the office routine, as nearly as possible put ourselves in the place of the clerks who wrote them and had to use them. Even then the task is not easy with the legal records. For their huge bulk, the absence of all form of reference in the roll save for the name of the county in the left margin, and—worst of all—their interminable length, make search arduous and uncertain. A single case may run through many rolls, and at the end we may be doubtful whether or no further search might not unearth further proceedings, except in those cases (a minority) in which a definite verdict is given.

IV

THE TRANSITION TO MODERN TIMES

BETWEEN say 1450 and 1550 a series of administra- Admini-
tive changes took place which together revolu- strative
changes
tionized the working of the central government. The 1450–1550.
old departments—the Chancery, the Privy Seal,
Exchequer, and Common Law Courts—went on,
outwardly but little changed. But in fact by the
death of Henry VIII the administrative centre of
gravity had been radically altered by the creation of
new machinery. We must not exaggerate the change,
for the old departments were themselves still capable
of that subtle and continuous modification which
marks all live administrations. But the future, even
though it was only imperfectly grasped at the time,
lay with the newly created supplementary offices. A
great field of research lies open to the student of these
changes, silently and almost unconsciously recorded
in the public records. In finance we find a new
Treasury System created, a change reflected in the
splendid series of the Declared Accounts, which
'rendered superfluous, without however abolishing the
old course' of the Exchequer. Similarly, in regard to
Law, new records crowd into the picture—the Proceedings of the Star Chamber and the Court of Requests, for example—without however superseding in
this instance, the old Common Law records. Religious
changes necessitated a new Court of Augmentations,

a Court of Tenths and First Fruits, and a series of commissions which grew into the Court of High Commission. Most revolutionary of all perhaps were the changes introduced into the central secretariat, by the rise of the Secretaries of State.

Rise of the Secretaries of State.
The King's Secretary, the Keeper of the Signet, was, we have seen, the head of the third successive secretariat evolved in the Middle Ages. In the century 1450–1550 it was settled that no further duplication was to occur, no further secretariats were to be formed: and that the Secretary was to supplant permanently the two still earlier and more dignified offices of the Chancery and the Privy Seal. The King's Secretary became the centre of the administrative machine; soon there were two, the King's two principal Secretaries; then the two principal Secretaries of State. All domestic and foreign business lay in their hands and so grew up—a vast new class of archives—the State Papers. They begin to develop into a large class quite suddenly about 1518. Thus the student who is studying Henry VII is still largely dependent upon the Chancery records, the student of Henry VIII relies far more upon the State Papers.

The State Papers.
The State Papers are a new form of public record: there is nothing like them in the Middle Ages. They are not the routine products of an office, but the intimate and miscellaneous correspondence of an official whose duties knew no fixed limits. In-letters, out-letters, drafts, reports, schedules, written for the most part on paper, of all shapes and sizes, they seem

never to have had any other arrangement than that
of the rough chronological order in which they are
still kept. Their importance cannot easily be exag-
gerated, and I do not think it wrong to say that they
make history possible in a fuller measure than ever
before. The veil that separates us from character and
personality in the Middle Ages is torn aside and with
the wider possibility of historical interpretation, the
possibilities of dispute and difference of opinion are
increased tenfold. The reason lies in the informal
character of these records. Men were now beginning
to put on to paper the ideas of the moment, the
thoughts and the gossip which in the Middle Ages
seldom passed the spoken word. A new technique is
required for dealing with this sort of material, and the
central interest of students leaves the history of institutions and turns to people.

The reverse of this startling development is seen Disap-
in the obsolescence of other records. The decline of pearance
of certain
the medieval King's Council and the slow decay of medieval
certain characteristic Chancery records created a gap archives.
in administrative function. The Proceedings of the
King's Council printed by Nicolas, end abruptly in
1461, and when a fresh series starts in 1540 they are
the records of a radically different organization, the
interval coinciding with the emergence of the King's
Secretaries. With their appearance as the virtual
administrative centre of English government is equally
connected the disappearance of the Charter Rolls
(which end in 8 Henry VIII) and of the Fine Rolls

(in 13 Charles I). Most curious of all is the change
which comes over the great series of the Close Rolls.
In the Middle Ages they had contained the writs
issued under the Great Seal·to sheriffs, escheators,
justices, and other royal servants—a complete administrative record of the central government. On the
back or dorse of the roll private persons from about
the middle of the thirteenth century had been accus-
tomed to have entered copies of various private deeds
for safe keeping. Gradually the number of letters
issued under the Great Seal decreased. Finally, in
Henry VIII's reign they cease and from that time
for centuries to come the face of the Close Roll
remained a blank while the back continued to be
used for the enrolment of private deeds. There could
hardly be a better example of the passing away of the
medieval system after the middle of the fifteenth century; one result of which was to leave the reigns of
Edward IV and Henry VII perhaps the worst 'docu-
mented' period since the beginning of the Chancery
enrolments in 1199.

The State   The growth of the State Papers involved the crea-
Paper   tion of a new office—the State Paper Office, founded
Office. in 1578. The first Clerk of the Papers was Dr. Thomas
Wilson, but it was his nephew and successor Sir
Thomas Wilson, who really organized the new depart-
ment. He, first, divided them into the two simple
classes—Foreign and Domestic, which persist to-day;
and he it was who insisted on the principle that State
Papers were *public* records. For already there was a

tendency on the part of officials to retain all such papers on retirement. This habit, which was not confined to the Secretaries of State, though checked, was never really stopped until the nineteenth century; and explains the large collection of public documents which are to-day in the Harleian and Cotton Collections in the British Museum, as well as such collections as those at Hatfield House and the 'Amherst' papers.

The State Papers are the archives of that immediate activity of the Secretary, which, even in the medieval period, was the most important part of his duties.[1] The lesser function of the Signet as a warrant for grants under the Great Seal, it must be borne in mind, survived the Middle Ages and the process became even more elaborate and cumbersome. The Clerks of the Signet developed in their turn into a department and another link was thus introduced into the chain which connected the original petition of the subject with the final instrument under the Great Seal. For the late sixteenth century and thenceforward until well into the nineteenth the diagram of the stages[2] must be amended as follows:

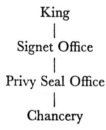

King
|
Signet Office
|
Privy Seal Office
|
Chancery

[1] Above, p. 31.

[2] Above, p. 28.

The separation of the Sovereign from the Signet is closely connected with the rise of two new offices of great constitutional importance—those of the Attorney-General and the Solicitor-General. The 'Law Officers of the Crown' became involved in the granting of all but the most routine 'Patents', and two new series of records grew up—warrants on paper to the Law Officers (or, in simple cases, to the Clerk of the Signet in attendance) to prepare a Bill for the king's signature, and a final warrant on parchment, the 'King's Bill', also signed by the king, which was sent to the Signet Office and supplied authority for the successive warrants to the Privy Seal, and thence to the Chancery as described above. The text of these, which was itself usually preceded by a report from one or both of the Law Officers on the propriety of making the proposed grant, began 'Our will and pleasure is that you forthwith prepare a Bill for our royal signature, to pass our Great Seal', and shortly set out the subject of the grant. The King's Bill contained the full text of the instrument, and (if endorsed to that effect) could become an 'immediate warrant' to the Chancery, thus eliminating the two intermediate stages of the Signet and Privy Seal. Care was taken, however, that even in these cases the substance of the Bill was entered in the Signet and Privy Seal 'Docquet' books. In this way the clerks secured their fees and the beneficiary was saved time but not money. The 'warrants to prepare a bill' and the 'King's Bills' were both signed by the

Law Officers, the Secretary of State, or other responsible officer before they received the king's signature.
They served as a protection to the Crown, which
could then fix responsibility on some definite person
and so could 'do no wrong'. This intricate procedure,
the final elaboration of the curious process of grants
under the Great Seal, lasted until 1857 when the
Clerks of the Signet were abolished, their work taken
over by the Home Office, and the whole process
greatly simplified.[1]

It is a remarkable fact that the country was
administered as late as 1782 by only two Secretaries
of State—one for the Northern, the other for the
Southern Department. In that year the Secretary
of State for the Northern Department became the
head of a new department—the Foreign Office, and
a little later in 1794 a Secretary of State for War was
appointed. Very curious is the growth of the Colonial
Office. In 1768 a Secretary of State for the Colonies
was appointed, but abolished in 1782 (after the loss
of the American Colonies), the work being transferred
to the Home Office. In 1794 the Colonies were transferred to the newly-formed Department of War, whose
chief bore the title of Secretary for the Department
of War and the Colonies. Finally, on the outbreak of
war with Russia in 1854, the Colonies received a
Secretary of State of their own.

It is unnecessary to trace farther the growth of

Increase in the number of the Secretaries of State.

---

[1] See *Notes on the Great Seal*, pp. 93 sqq., for details of the full
modern procedure.

The Modern Departmental System. the modern departments. Modern bureaucracy has grown from the multiplication of departments, most of which have in time received a Secretary of State as their chief. The new departments are not so closely correlated and interrelated as those of the Middle Ages. What co-ordination there is of these different activities is secured partly by the growth of the Cabinet system, partly by a common submission of all other departments to Treasury control: so that the permanent Secretary of the Treasury is now officially called the head of the Civil Service. Some of these departments, e.g. the War Office, represent the devolution of functions once directly discharged by the Royal Household. The Treasury is nothing more than the ancient office of Lord High Treasurer in Commission, an office which had gone 'out of court' as early as the twelfth century. Similarly, the Admiralty Board has taken over the powers of the Lord High Admiral, an office which remained in the Household for at least three centuries later. Other offices—for example, that of the Treasury Solicitor—have their origin in post-medieval times, while certain more recent war ministries disappear, leaving only tons of paper behind.

Departmental Records. From the point of view of their records it is important to remember that each department still has full control over its own records. Unlike those of the Chancery and Exchequer and the Law Courts they are not under the control of the Master of the Rolls. By a purely voluntary agreement many departments have taken advantage of the permissory act of 1838 to place their archives in charge of the Master of the Rolls at the Record Office. But the arrangement of these records is retained by the department. This, we shall see later, is important for the researcher. Some departments, like the Post Office, have never taken advantage of this offer, and still retain their own records. A summary of the Departmental Records preserved in the Public Record Office is contained in volume ii of *Giuseppi's Guide*.

A more detailed list of the records of each department is given in the series of *Lists and Indexes*. Underlying all the obvious and superficial differences there is an essential similarity between these modern archives and those of the older, medieval depart- The
ments. The Foreign Office (*Lists and Indexes*, no. lii), Foreign
Office
prior to 1906, may be taken as a typical example of Records.
one of these newer administrations. Its archives, if we exclude certain private collections (e.g. the private papers of Stratford Canning, F.O. 352) and the archives of occasional commissions (e.g. America: North-West Boundaries, F.O. 302), fall into two main divisions:

1. Records accumulated at Whitehall.
2. Embassy and Consular Archives.

The largest class in the first of these divisions is that of *General Correspondence*, arranged according to countries (e.g. America, F.O. 5; France, F.O. 27) and classified under each country as (*a*) Correspondence with the English ambassadors in that country, (*b*) Correspondence with Consuls, (*c*) Correspondence with Foreign Ministers in London. In each of these three classes the correspondence is divided into in-letters and out-letters and the distinction carefully noted in the *List*. Subsidiary to this *fonds* of correspondence relating to particular countries is the correspondence relating to many countries on general and miscellaneous subjects (Great Britain and General, F.O. 83) and a class devoted to the Slave Trade (F.O. 84). These are purely artificial classes, abstracted from the main body of *General Correspondence*, since the letters in them by *provenance* also belong to the correspondence with particular countries. An elaborate index to all the correspondence is supplied by the *Registers*, still kept for the most part at the Foreign Office. There are besides two other large classes of a wholly different kind, viz. Treaties (F.O. 93 and 94) and Accounts (F.O. 366); and the inevitable *Miscellanea* (F.O. 95 and 96).

The Embassy and Consular Archives, the second great division, are similarly arranged under each country. Here again the chief *fonds* is that of *Correspondence*, the volumes of in-letters and out-letters being distinguished, with two minor classes of *Registers* and *Sub-Consulates*.

In this arrangement the 'out-letters' are in essence no more than the Chancery enrolments, while the in-letters correspond to the Chancery files. In both cases there are the same untidy little classes that will not fit into the main scheme; and there is the same kind of interrelation between classes. Thus, for example, the Embassy records will supply the *originals* (often initialled) of many of the out-letters, preserved at Whitehall only in copies; and the two classes must be used together. But what we miss in the modern departments is any organic connexion with the records of other departments. The size of modern bureaucracy has involved extreme specialization; and this in turn means separateness. The Cabinet system, which has preserved an undivided sovereign power in government, has failed to preserve the unifying force of a single will and purpose in administration. The lack of any directing centre is a chief defect in modern bureaucracy; and from the point of view of the archivist, the chief interest of the governmental experiments in Italy and Germany lies in the reaction towards the medieval system of centralizing the whole administration in a personal sovereign.

I cannot forbear to add the ingenious device by which administrative continuity in these departments has been combined with the frequent changes of ministers under the Parliamentary system, viz. the creation of a professional, salaried, *permanent* civil service which goes on whatever government is in power. In each department its head is the Permanent Secretary, who must never be confused with the Secretary of State. The latter is more in the public eye and is supposed to originate policy.

This last development of a paid and now pensioned

Civil Service recruited by examination is of fundamental importance in the history of English administration, and therefore of the public records. It made possible a reorganization of the whole Civil Service and the final abolition of an army of useless officials and worn out offices, which had defied the efforts of centuries to reform them. The whole history of administration in England, as in France, is bound up with the fact that an office once created became a vested interest, almost a franchise or liberty. A system of patronage governed the grant and reversion of all these posts, which might almost be described as lay 'benefices' or 'livings'. For example:

'The Master of the Rolls,' Sir Henry Maxwell Lyte tells us,[1] 'had the sole right of appointing the Six Clerks, the three Clerks of the Petty Bag, the two Examiners, the seven Clerks of the Rolls Chapel, and the Usher, the Crier, and the Door-keeper of the Court of Chancery, and, in the earlier part of the seventeenth century, most of the officers had to pay him for their places. Lord Bruce, who was Master of the Rolls from May 1603 to January 1611, received £12,000 for three of the Six Clerkships, vacated by death, and £2,200 for three others, vacated by surrender. A clerkship of the Petty Bag, vacated by death, yielded him £1,500, while two others and an examinership, vacated by surrender, yielded him £300 apiece.'

The sale of offices was forbidden by an ordinance of Cromwell, as Lord Protector, in 1654, but 'this

[1] *Historical Notes on the Great Seal*, pp. 6–7.

salutary order was entirely ignored', and the practice continued throughout the eighteenth century.

This system, which to some extent explains the endless duplication of offices in the past, was ruthlessly scrapped in the nineteenth century; and with it passed the system of overlapping, competing jurisdictions to which it had given rise. In this respect it was utterly different from that earlier transition which remoulded the administration in Tudor times. With the vast changes of the nineteenth century the development to modern times was complete, the result being that there is a greater difference between the archives of 1780 and 1880 than there is between those of 1780 and the later Middle Ages. It remains to be seen whether the new system will maintain the comparative stability of the older administration— for with all its faults it had this great merit.

V

THE APPROACH TO RESEARCH

Public Records in print. THE intention of this last section is to give some practical help and information to the student who has already learnt some history, who has perhaps done some 'research', but has not yet actually worked on the original documents. A great many of the public records have already been published, and the printed material is the natural link between a general acquaintance with administrative history and the real 'game of research'.

The bibliography of public records in print is a very great and ever-growing difficulty. The records published by our predecessors are the foundation and starting-point of all our work. It is customary and proper to pay a tribute to the men and institutions who, by the texts they published, have lightened our labours. Yet from another point of view they are a millstone round our necks, increasing the burden of mere knowledge to be accumulated from print before further progress is possible. Research is thus a greater strain upon each generation of those who pursue it, and for the same reasons becomes, and must still become, more and more specialized and minute. The researcher on manuscripts has always to be on his guard that the significant document he believes himself to have discovered has not already appeared in print. The Public Record Office index of public records already printed (mentioned below)[1] is a real help, and I would like here to suggest that its systematic completion is a most urgent need of modern research. It is a task which (in this country) can only be undertaken by private enterprise and financed by private funds. But it is a very necessary one, if we wish to prevent constant overlapping and the doing of good work twice over.

The difficulties would be infinitely greater than they are but for the publications of records by H.M. Government. For well over a century the task of either printing in full or calendaring the national records has been shouldered by the State, and on the whole the work has been done very well. For the publications have been on a large scale, simple in arrangement and systematic in scope. These are cardinal virtues, and it is not too much to say that the Government Publications have saved research from the sheer chaos which would have resulted from the publication of the main classes of public records by private effort. For with few exceptions the Government has avoided the perhaps necessary evil of private effort—the publication of short selections, extracts, and snippets. *The Official Publications.*

A short guide to the official publications, called *List 24*, is supplied (free) by the Stationery Office, and revised in successive issues at frequent intervals. It is an invaluable work of reference to a vast body of printed records, the general scope of which the student must carry in his head. *List 24.*

[1] p. 84.

The idea that the Government should finance the
publication of the national records has grown up
slowly, almost imperceptibly, since the sixteenth century. Matthew Parker's books at Lambeth, collected
with the aid of the Privy Council, have been described
as the 'Foreign Office Library of the Elizabethan
Period', and his publications—Gildas, Asser, Ælfric,
Matthew Paris, and Walsingham—were at least 'semi-
official'. But perhaps we may take Thomas Rymer's
edition of the *Foedera* (1704–13) as the first large
experiment in publication of the national records.
The suggestion apparently came from Lord Somers,
and Rymer was appointed editor by royal warrant
and given facilities to search all the public reposi-
tories. He was also paid, though very badly paid, for
his work by the Government, and he died in poverty.
For a few years a general interest was aroused in the
state of the public records. In 1719 a committee of
the House of Lords reported on the neglect into which
they had fallen and on their scandalous custody; and
in 1732 a committee of the House of Commons made
a similar report on the Cottonian Collection after the
fire at Ashburnham House. But nothing further was
done about publication until 1767, when the printing
of the *Rolls of Parliament* was undertaken by Parliament. This was followed in 1783 by the publication
of Domesday Book, *jubente rege augustissimo Georgio
tertio*—so well done that it has never been superseded.
These volumes mark an advance upon Rymer's *Foedera*, or at least a change of plan, for now the Govern-

ment for the first time assumed official responsibility for publication and bore the whole cost.

The public conscience was roused at last about the national records, and in 1800 the *First Commission on the Public Records* published an exhaustive report, which is still the starting-point of any investigation of their history. From the point of view of publication, no less than of custody, the year 1800 marks a turning-point in the history of the public records. During the years 1800–37 no less than six commissions upon the records were set up, and a large number of volumes were published. *[Publications of the Record Commissioners, 1800–37.]*

The distinguishing mark of the books published in this period is the *record type* in which they are printed. By a series of typographical conventions—originally devised for the publication of the Rolls of Parliament and Domesday Book—an attempt was made to represent in print an absolutely faithful reproduction of the original manuscript. The texts so printed, it must be said, were on the whole very well done, many of them by extremely able men like Palgrave and Joseph Hunter, who edited the earliest Pipe Roll. On the other hand, no settled plan governed the selection of what was to be printed, so that the publications of this period are a most miscellaneous group, the start of many great enterprises, none of which, except the Statutes of the Realm and the *Rotuli Scotiae*, were brought to completion. A simultaneous beginning, for example, was made upon the three most important classes of Chancery enrolments—the Charter, Patent, and Close Rolls—but carried no farther than the end of John's reign or (in the case of the Close Rolls) the early years of Henry III. Palgrave, again, published a single volume of early *Curia Regis* Rolls: there was a volume of early *Fines*, and a few volumes of early Miscellaneous Rolls, chosen almost at random. These examples, typical of the whole, illustrate the one common feature of the publications of this period, viz. the (very natural) absorption of the editors in the medieval records. They were beginning at the beginning.

The sixth and last of the Record Commissions came to an end in 1837. The publications had been so exorbitantly expensive as to become almost a public scandal. With them disappeared the pedantic use of *record type*, perhaps on grounds of expense. The next year the Public Record Office Act was passed, provision being made for the issue of future volumes under the supervision of the Master of the Rolls. But for nearly twenty years there were no further publications, except the annual reports of the Deputy Keeper of the Records, many of which, however, contain valuable appendixes and lists of documents. Then in 1856 began a new era in publication, and for the next thirty years far more public money was available for printing than ever before, or, alas, ever since. It was a golden age for editors. Stubbs, for instance, received more than £500 for editing the two volumes of Benedict of Peterborough in the Rolls Series, and £1,200 for the four volumes of *Roger of Hoveden*. In

The Public Record Office Act (1838).

The Second Period of Official Publications 1856–86).

the same period the great depository in Chancery Lane was built and the *Public Record Office* came into existence. Two most important series began and were energetically carried on in this period.

1. *The Rolls Series,* modelled upon Pertz's *Monumenta Germaniae Historica.*

The Rolls Series was for the most part concerned to print the literary sources of history, and it should be added of medieval history. There were, however, a few cartularies of religious houses, e.g. Abingdon, Gloucester, Evesham: a few more of official correspondence, e.g. Royal Letters (Shirley) 2 vols., the correspondence of Henry IV (Hingeston)—vol. ii being suppressed and destroyed after it had been printed off!—and of Thomas Bekington (Williams): one was a Parliament Roll edited by Maitland, and the greater part of the Red Book of the Exchequer was edited by Dr. Hall.

The value of the Rolls Series to English history can hardly be overrated, but it suffered from the absence of any methodical plan or order of publication, and the scholarship shown in the editing was often defective. The series was originally intended to be focused round Sir Thomas Duffus Hardy's *Descriptive Catalogue of Manuscripts Relating to the History of Great Britain and Ireland.* But only the first three volumes of this useful work were published; and in fact it did little to determine the selection of material to be printed. The copy left by Hardy at his death, which covered the fourteenth century, proved to be too fragmentary to print. It was, however, bound up and placed on the shelves of the Literary Search Room, and is therefore still available for reference. In execution the Rolls Series is very uneven: no level standard of competence, not even a low standard, was maintained. Some volumes, e.g. those of Luard, Stubbs, and Maitland, are admirable; many are more or less competent; some are wholly inadequate. Soon after Sir Henry Maxwell Lyte's appointment as Deputy Keeper in 1886 the series was discontinued, and has never, unfortunately, been revived.

2. *The Calendars of State Papers.*

The Calendars of State Papers. The Rolls Series, we have seen, were based on the German *Monumenta*. The *Calendars* similarly arose out of 'some very able reports which M. Guizot, as the Minister of Public Instruction, has addressed to the King of the French'. As early as 1825 a series of extracts printed *in extenso* from the State Papers of Henry VIII had been begun, and eleven volumes had been issued. These, however, were the work not of the Record Commissioners but of the strictly departmental *State Papers* Commission. The value of the post-Reformation State Papers as historical material now began to be realized. The State Paper Office was amalgamated in 1854 with the Record Office and the series of Calendars begun in 1856 with the volume of *Edward VI, Mary and Elizabeth* (1547–80). From that day to this the enormous task has been carried steadily on and is still barely half finished. To-day it may be stated roughly that the Domestic and Colonial State Papers have been calendared to about the reign of George I, while the calendar of State Papers Foreign has hardly advanced beyond the Armada. With these may be grouped the valuable collection of Treasury Books (1660–1718), and (1729–45); certain series of modern records, like the Privy Council Register and the Journal of the Board of Trade and Plantations which have been printed in full; and a large number of volumes based on Foreign archives, Spain, Venice, Milan, the Papal Archives at Rome; and Round's *Calendar of Documents preserved in France (918–1206)*.

A new period in the history of Government publica- The Third
tions, particularly of medieval publications, begins Period of
with the succession of Sir Henry Maxwell Lyte to the Publica-
Deputy Keepership in 1886. The series of 'modern' tions, 1886–
calendars was continued and even extended, but the Official
Rolls Series, as we have seen, was abandoned, and the
financial saving on this side made possible the extension of the 'calendar system' to the medieval records. Hitherto, medieval texts had been printed *in extenso*, or in some cases, e.g. the *Rotulorum Originalium . . . Abbreviatio*, as extracts or selections. Indeed, it is likely that the idea of an English summary of Latin documents, even the 'barbarous' Latin of the Middle Ages, would have shocked the generation of the Record Commission. Sir Henry now broke through this prejudice and, to the incalculable gain of students, began

The the great series of calendars of the medieval Chancery
Medieval Rolls—the Charter, Patent, Close, and Fine Rolls,
Calendars. which have been carried on by his successors. At
the present time the whole of the Charter Rolls have
now been calendared: the Patent Rolls are calendared
to the year 1563, the Close Rolls to 1468, and the
Fine Rolls to the reign of Edward IV.

The calendars of the Charter and Patent Rolls were
begun at the point where the Record Commissioners
who, it will be remembered, had printed the rolls *in
extenso*, stopped. The Fine Rolls were merely calendared from the year 1272 onwards; but the Close
Rolls have now been printed in full to 1272, the
accession of Edward I being chosen as the starting-
point of the calendars. The policy of abandoning the
full publication of the medieval records, which was
criticized at the time, has been fully vindicated. The
execution of the calendars is open to some legitimate
criticism, particularly as regards certain omissions,
e.g. the witnesses to charters in the Charter Roll
Calendar, but no one to-day denies the wisdom of
the plan which has made accessible in little more
than a generation so much of the state papers of the
Middle Ages. It was in fact the logical completion
of the calendars of modern state papers to which these
rolls are really analogous.

The calendar system has been extended with suc-
cess to other medieval records, e.g. the six volumes
of *Feudal Aids* and seventeen volumes of *Inquisitions
post mortem*. But the medieval Exchequer Records still

remain almost untouched, and will sooner or later have to be dealt with, particularly the Memoranda Rolls. At the present moment we depend almost entirely upon the admirable publications of a private society—the Pipe Roll Society—for our knowledge of perhaps the finest financial organization of the Middle Ages. The legal records are similarly unique in their own sphere and have been equally neglected, except the very early ones which have been printed *in extenso*, under Sir Cyril Flower's editorship, into the reign of Henry III. One other enterprise of Sir Henry Maxwell Lyte deserves particular mention. This is the *Book of Fees*, or scholarly re-edition of the *Testa de Neville*, planned by himself and carried through under his close supervision. It is perhaps the most important of the records printed *in extenso* in this period, and it has a magnificent index.

It remains to mention one other innovation of Sir Henry Maxwell Lyte—the Series of Lists and Indexes, issued in folio, which runs to more than fifty volumes. They include both the great modern departments, like the Treasury and War Office, and the medieval courts of Chancery, Exchequer, and the Common Law Courts. By their admirable arrangement they give within reasonable compass a rapid and effective survey of the records in each class, generally distinguishing each volume and giving a rough idea of the date it covers.

One obstacle, generally regarded as of all the most

Palaeo-severe, still lies in the path of the researcher—the
graphy. preliminary difficulty of deciphering the documents.
In the Middle Ages and in many series far into modern
times the language of archives is either Latin or
French; and even when English is used the script is
apt at first sight to make one almost despair. This is
an illusion. A few weeks', in some cases a few days'
study, of the two standard text-books will enable any-
one with a good knowledge of elementary Latin to
get the sense of any ordinary document. To make
an accurate transcript is another matter. The court
hand in which they are written is a legitimate, if sub-
ordinate, branch of palaeography with its own rules
and its distinctive alphabets; but differing fundament-
ally from text or book hand in its purely utilitarian
object. The aim of the scribe was to write well if
possible, but at all costs to write quickly; and what
he wrote was rarely revised or examined. It follows
that in difficult passages purely palaeographical con-
siderations—contractions, abbreviations, and letter-
forms—hardly carry the same weight as in text hand.
We must give rather more weight to the mind and
intention of the scribe. And for the very reason that
formal rules tend to fail us so quickly, proportionately
more weight attaches to sheer experience in reading.
In fact a long apprenticeship is required before the
documents can be transcribed with real exactitude.
And so, roughly speaking, it comes to this, that the
early stages of court hand are less difficult, while high
proficiency is more difficult, than in the study of book

hands. A great deal, however, of archive palaeography consists of common forms and when this is
fully grasped the chief difficulties are apt to lie in the
correct reading of proper names and in the forms of
capital letters. In any event the merest rudiments are
all that is necessary to make a start in the Search
Room of the Record Office; and there are many
who have begun on the documents without even this
modest equipment.

How exactly should the student transcribe his
documents, whether for private use or for publication? This is a vexed question, on which there is no
general agreement either in theory or in practice. In
my opinion the basic consideration is this—that no
printed text can fully represent, and still less super-
sede, the original document: sometimes even a photograph is inadequate and may mislead us. In the last
resort nothing can replace the study of the original.
A century ago the Record Commission in its publications tried by means of 'record type' virtually to
reproduce the document, with all its abbreviations.
This special type was very costly, very difficult to
read, and quite useless when a real palaeographical
difficulty occurred. Later the Early English Text
Society made another well-meant attempt to achieve
the impossible by extending abbreviations and printing the extensions in italics. To-day there even seems
to be a tendency in printing English texts to revert
to the principles of record type. But all these devices
are open to the same objection. They are costly,

*The
Transcrip-
tion of
Records.*

unpleasant to read, and impossible to quote. Above all they are unscientific, since they have a delusive air of giving us those *minutiae* which in fact the original can alone supply. The written word and the printed word are, in fact, totally different things; and we must take care not to make the latter actually more difficult to read than the former! The student will find in the practice of the Public Record Office publications, based on generations of experience in printing, a good practical model on which to base his own transcripts. These texts normally 'extend' all abbreviations about which there is no reasonable doubt—that is the vast majority. No special type is required and no italics. Where there is uncertainty the letters of the original are printed followed by a superior comma or tick, thus ', leaving such difficulties to be settled (if possible) by a sight of the original or of a photograph. Nor is there any attempt made industriously to reproduce the capital letters of the manuscript or even (in most cases) its punctuation. The worst that can be said of such a method is that it puts a heavy, though legitimate, responsibility upon the editor or transcriber of the document—the responsibility of knowing his job and of making up his mind.

The First Visit to the Public Record Office. With a decent knowledge of the historical background to the records, and a slight acquaintance with palaeography, the student is in a position to make a start on the original documents. The first hours spent in a library are nearly always unprofitable, partly on account of the newcomer's ignorance of its organization; even more perhaps because he is dazed by the strangeness of things. He is apt to feel stupid and act accordingly, and valuable hours are wasted. In the Public Record Office these initial difficulties are very much enhanced by its inevitably complex and technical arrangement. Like the history of institutions, the Public Record Office cannot be mastered—can scarcely be approached—without an effort. But the period of bewilderment may be shortened and time may be saved by a preliminary knowledge of the organization of the Search Rooms and the routine there followed.

The only qualification necessary for research in the Public Record Office is a Reader's Ticket, which can be obtained from the Secretary. This can be done in writing—there is no need for a personal visit—and as a form has to be filled up and signed by some one who knows the applicant, it is a wise precaution to write a week or so before one wants to begin working. The ticket once obtained, it may be added, is valid indefinitely and needs no renewal. A student not of British birth must obtain a letter of introduction from his Embassy to the Foreign Office, which will be forwarded in due course to the Public Record Office. *Readers' Tickets.*

Two Search Rooms are provided for the public, called respectively the Literary or Round Search Room (it actually has sixteen sides), and the Legal Search Room. Either room may be used, but the Literary Search Room is the more convenient for all except those who wish to examine the most recent *The Literary and Legal Search Rooms.*

legal records, because of the careful series of reference books with which it is provided. It is particularly valuable for the medieval researcher.

The Literary Search Room, which is not large, is well lighted by a glass roof. Officers of the department preside on conspicuous raised desks, assisted by two or three highly trained officials whom the most unfathomable ignorance will leave unmoved. The prudent researcher, having provided himself with the correct title (and if possible, reference) of *some* document relevant to his inquiry, will at once get in touch The with the officer in charge of the room. He will be System of shown how to fill in the necessary ticket for his docu-Reference. ment, and the place to put it. He will also learn, in these first moments, something of the methods of reference. These, which are designed to accelerate the production of documents, consist broadly speaking of a capital letter, or two, indicating the class or archive group, followed by a number, which stands for the subdivision within the group. For example, E/101 refers to the series of Accounts Various in the office of the King's Remembrancer, a subdivision of the Exchequer (E); or C/81 is the correct reference to the *Warrants for the Great Seal*, Series I, a subdivision of the Chancery records. A second number gives the precise document or file in the series. Thus E/101/96 will produce a box containing documents referring to the Council (Wages and Diet). Finally, a third number distinguishes the various pieces in this box. For example, E/101/96/8 is the correct reference for a small file of two membranes giving the accounts for the Council breakfasts in the forty-first year of Edward III.

This is not very difficult to master, and there is a great saving of time and trouble to all concerned, if the reader gives the right references in the right way. It must be borne in mind that these symbols, mere devices 'to assist production', are not valid references for published work, which should quote the title of the documents referred to, either in full or by an intelligible abbreviation. A wise custom of the Department encourages the reader to put in tickets for the documents he requires next day before he goes away. They will then be waiting for him when he arrives in the morning. Time can be saved too by sending a post card addressed to the Officer in charge of the Literary Search Room, specifying the documents that he will require on any given date ahead.

On a first visit, there will naturally be a pause while the document is being fetched. If he is not too busy the Officer in charge will now direct the researcher to the invaluable class of summary printed *Lists and Indexes* and a large collection of other references to almost every class of records. These are arranged in presses round the walls, under the various courts or departments, as shown in the diagram. This arrangement is rigidly adhered to, so that books which contain lists or calendars to more than a single class have been divided, the relevant portions being rebound and placed upon the appropriate shelf. Each press

The Reference Books.

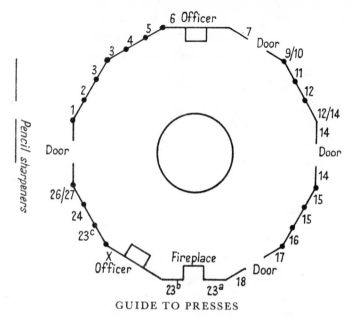

GUIDE TO PRESSES

1. State Papers. Henry VIII.
   State Papers. Foreign.
2. State Papers. Domestic.
3. Departmental Lists.
4. Special Collections.
   Gifts. Transcripts.
5. Exchequer: Augumentation
   Office. F.F.
6. Exchequer: T.R.: L.R.:
   L.T.R. Exchequ. of Receipt.
7. Exchequer: K.R.
9/10. Legal Courts, &c.
11. Common Pleas: Indexes
    to Fines.
12. Parliament and Council.
14. Reference: *Foedera*, &c.
15. Reference: D.K.'s Reports,
    Calendars issued by other
    Archives.

16. Reference: Chronology, &c.
17. Reference: Languages, Law.
18. Reference: Palaeography,
    Atlases. Topography: Local
    Publications.
23*a*. Close Rolls: Printed Calen-
    dars.
23*b*. Patent Roll, Charter Roll,
    Fine Roll, and other printed
    Calendars.
23*c*. Patent Roll and Close Roll:
    MS. Indexes.
24. Inquisitions: printed Calen-
    dars; and other Chancery
    lists.
26. Scotland and Ireland.
27. Wales, Lancaster, and the
    Palatinates.
X. Card Catalogue of Records in
    print.

Note: Other means of reference are kept in presses in the Legal Search
Room and in the South Room.

is numbered and labelled with the name of the class
and each volume is numbered within the press.

The printed *Lists and Indexes*—the starting-point of
research upon any particular class—naturally form
only a small fraction of the books on these shelves.
There are in addition more detailed inventories of
subsections of records in each class, lists now obso-
lete with 'Keys' giving the present references, catalogues extracted from the Deputy Keepers' Reports,
printed archives, like the Red Book of the Exchequer,
two presses of general reference books—date books,
dictionaries, peerages, and so on, and finally, a complete collection of the printed *Calendars* issued by the
department.

The bulk of these various methods of reference, The class
which fill a dozen presses, may well seem over- of
'Indexes'.
whelming. Yet they are but the first line of attack
upon the records. Besides these there is, among the
records themselves, a huge array of volumes which
are in the nature of indexes and abstracts, made by
the various departments, and therefore at once themselves archives and a means of access to archives.
Nothing gives one so just a conception of the vast
concentration of records at Chancery Lane as these
14,000 volumes, which fill three great rooms, adjacent
to the Literary Search Room. They are numbered
straight through and form by themselves a great *class*
of Indexes. This Index class is correlated, with the
other means of reference provided in the Literary
Search Room, by means of a great eight-volume

Catalogue of Lists and Indexes, now at last completed, copies of which are deposited in the British Museum, the Institute of Historical Research, and the Bodleian Library. The Catalogue directs the searcher to all the known means of reference to every section of the Public Records.

Distinction between the records of the Courts and the Departmental Records. I have already referred (p. 61) to the distinction between the old records of the Chancery, Exchequer, and Law Courts, which are in the custody of the Master of the Rolls and the later departmental records which are merely under his superintendence. The distinction is of practical importance, for each department reserves the right to fix a date after which its records are not open to public inspection. This is in most cases 1902, but it varies as can be seen by studying the list of departmental records which is hung up in the Literary Search Room. Records of later date can only be seen by special permission of the department concerned. This is carried to extreme lengths in the case of the Office of Works, none of whose records are open to inspection except by special permission of the First Commissioner. Finally, it should be noted, that all legal records after 1842 can only be seen on payment of a fee. This regulation is the *raison d'être* of the Legal Search Room, where only they can be produced to the public.

The Card Catalogue of Public Records printed. The danger of reprinting records already published is a constant worry and sometimes a nightmare of the historical student. To meet this, a card catalogue of records in print is kept in the Literary

Search Room. It now contains 40,000 cards and, though still far from complete, is of very great value.

There are also catalogues of seals and of maps; while in another department is the immense catalogue of manors compiled by the Master of the Rolls Committee on Manorial Records.

The study of administration has lately become almost a separate branch of history. Whatever one's view of this development may be, a certain acquaintance with administrative history is necessary for modern research. It can hardly be approached otherwise. For the Public Records are now arranged, so far as possible, under the various offices and departments which produced them. These offices, at least until the nineteenth century, were all parts of a single closely interrelated administrative system. To use them intelligently it is therefore necessary to understand the working of this system in general, and the routine of the departments with which the researcher is concerned. This is no easy matter, for the various departments were undergoing a process of continuous internal change, so that a 'live' class of records will with time become merely formal, even though it may last for centuries. Thus the Close Rolls, a true record of thirteenth-century administration, have already lost much of their importance by the fourteenth century with the use of the Privy Seal. Similarly, the use of the Jury of twelve men to inquire into the lands of deceased tenants-in-chief and the age of the heir which at some early period must have been a living institution degenerated slowly into 'common form'. The researcher has thus not merely to grasp the interaction of departments; he must as well judge the living value of his record at any particular time. He has thus a double motive for closely studying the actual process of administration.

Nor is this enough. Time, which has played havoc with many of the older *fonds* of our archives, has in some degree disturbed almost all of them. A knowledge of the history of the public records—or the classes relevant to the work in hand—is therefore also necessary. For this information the great class of Indexes is of special value, while much can be learnt from the Deputy Keeper's Reports, the Report of the First Record Commission (1800) and such books as Palgrave's *Kalendars and Inventories of the Exchequer*. In this way the original provenance of 'lost' documents can be determined, and the primitive grouping of classes now separated. The real starting-point of research is in short to fix the original arrangement of the records we are using.

The official *Guide* to the Public Records presupposes and requires this kind of approach to research, although the beginner will often get a useful hint from the older books of Thomas and Scargill-Bird with their subject arrangement. But for various reasons certain classes cannot be fitted into the structure of the modern *Guide*. The most important, as I have mentioned, is the *Special Collections* (pp. 339–47).

The chief of these—and they are of great importance—are:

Ancient Correspondence
Ancient Petitions
Court Rolls
Hundred Rolls
Ministers' Accounts
Papal Bulls
Rentals and Surveys

Special Collections.

All are artificial classes and for each (except the Hundred Rolls) there is a summary in the *Lists and Indexes Series*.

There are also the Documents presented to or deposited in the Public Record Office (pp. 348–51) which, according to the practice of the office, are not absorbed into the main collection; and there is too a large and valuable collection of transcripts (pp. 352–4) from Paris, Rome, and other places. Lastly, it is useful for two kinds of documents to abandon the departmental classification, viz. Ancient Deeds and Monastic Cartularies.

The Public Record Office contains many thousands of Ancient Deeds. Though they belong to various departments—to the Chancery, to the various branches of the Exchequer (K.R., Augmentation Office, Treasury of the Receipt, Land Revenue), to the Palatinate of Chester and the Duchy of Lancaster—they form in fact a single great collection, for their immediate provenance is in most cases purely accidental. Six volumes of a catalogue of Ancient Deeds have been published and a great many more are catalogued

Ancient Deeds.

though still unpublished. In addition to these should be mentioned vols. 29–54 of the Miscellaneous Books of the Augmentation Office, which are nothing more than scrap-books of original charters not included in the general series.

Books and Cartularies. Reference was made above to the Chancery Miscellanea, a much larger class than the name would suggest. Several other courts or departments have similar great collections of Miscellanea and Miscellaneous Books, too various for further classification, e.g. the King's Remembrancer's Department, the Augmentation Office, the Treasury of the Receipt, and the Duchy of Lancaster. A good summary of the contents of the Miscellanea of each of these departments is given in *Giuseppi's Guide*. Taken together they contain a fine series of monastic cartularies and similar books, the chief of which are:

Miscellaneous Books (Augmentation Office) vols. 55–63, Monastic Cartularies.

„   „   (King's Remembrancer) vols. 16–29, Monastic Cartularies.

„   „   (Duchy of Lancaster) vols. 1–10, Monastic Cartularies.

„   „   (Treasury of the Receipt) vol. 265, Cartulary of St. Mary's-without-Bishopsgate; 268, Stapleton's Calendar; 274, 275, Liber A and Liber B—important collections of Papal Bulls and other diplomatic documents of the reigns of Henry III and Edward I.

APPENDIX I

List of Books and References

A FULL list of all texts, calendars, &c., published by H.M. Government will be found in *List 24*; while the brief introductions to the various *Lists and Indexes* supply indispensable information about the classes of documents with which they deal. For the history of the Public Records there is a good bibliography in the *Report of the Royal Commission on the Public Records* (1912), vol. i (part ii), pp. 164–8. The publications of the *British Records Association* are indispensable for local and private records. For the history of administration, Tout's *Chapters* is invaluable for bibliographical references as well as for the facts. The publications of the Selden Society are the obvious starting-point for the study of legal records, and the *Bulletin of the Institute of Historical Research* is important for every aspect of archives, British and foreign. In the following list, which begins (in general) about the year 1199, works of special importance for those beginning research are marked with an asterisk.

GENERAL. A.

Calendar of Inquisitions, Miscellaneous. Preface to vol. i. London, 1916.

Calendar of Inquisitions, Hen. VII. Preface to vol. i. London, 1898.

Encyclopaedia Britannica, art. 'Records'.

*Giuseppi, M. S. *A Guide to the Manuscripts preserved in the Public Record Office.* Vol. i, Legal Records, &c. Vol. ii, State Paper Office, Public Departments. H.M. Stationery Office, 1923–4.

Hall, Hubert. *A Repertory of British Archives.* Part I: England. London, 1920.

—— *Studies in English Official Historical Documents.* Part I. Cambridge, 1908.

Hall, Hubert. *Formula Book of English Historical Docume.* I–II. Cambridge, 1908–9.

Holtzmann, Walther. 'Das englische Archivwesen' in *Archivalische Zeitschrift*, 3. Folge, 6. Band. Munich.

> A stimulating, if critical, description of English archive arrangements including the Public Record Office.

—— *Papsturkunden in England.* Vol. i. Berlin, 1930.

> Contains a valuable account of the material relating to the monasteries preserved in the Public Record Office.

Jenkinson, Hilary, and Mills, Mabel H. 'Rolls from a Sheriff's Office of the Fourteenth Century.' *E.H.R.* xliii (1928).

Jenkinson, Sir Hilary. *Guide to the Public Records.* Part I: Introductory. H.M. Stationery Office, 1949.

*Johnson, Charles. *The Public Record Office.* (Helps to Students of History.) S.P.C.K.

> The best short summary of the principal classes of Records.

Lyte, Sir H. C. Maxwell. *Catalogue of . . . the Public Record Office Museum.* H.M. Stationery Office, 1933.

**List of Record Publications* (*List 24*). H.M. Stationery Office, 1951.
> Indispensable.

Pike, L. O. *The Public Records and the Constitution.* London, 1907.

Record Commission: *Report from the Select Committee appointed to inquire into the state of the Public Records.* 1800.

> The best starting-point for the history of Public Records.

Report of the Royal Commission on the Public Records, 1912–1919.

'Report on Editing Historical Documents.' *Bulletin of the Inst. of Hist. Research*, vol. i, no. 1, and vol. iii, no. 7.

Satow, Sir Ernest M. *Guide to Diplomatic Practice.* 2 vols. London, 1917.

Scargill-Bird, S. R. *Guide to the Public Records.* 1st ed. 1891; 2nd ed. 1896; 3rd ed. 1908.

Thomas, F. S. *History of the State Paper Office with a view of the documents deposited therein.* London, 1849.

—— *Handbook to the Public Records.* London, 1853.

*Thompson, A. H. Hamilton. *Parish History and Records.* (Helps to Students of History.) S.P.C.K., 1915.

> The best small book on the value and use of the Public Records for local history.

*Tout, T. F. *Chapters in the Administrative History of England.*
6 vols. Manchester, 1920–33.

> Invaluable for the history of the Exchequer, Chancery,
> and Household from the Norman Conquest to 1399.

GENERAL. B.

Crump, C. G. *The Logic of History.* (Helps to Students of
History.) S.P.C.K.

—— 'A Note on the Criticism of Records.' *Bulletin of the John
Rylands Library,* vol. viii (1924).

*—— *History and Historical Research.* George Routledge, 1928.
> Good advice for those beginning research.

Edwards, Edward. *Libraries and Founders of Libraries, &c.* 1865.
> Pp. 211–326 contain the history of the Public Records.

Johnson, Charles. *The Care of Documents.* (Helps to Students of
History.) S.P.C.K.

*—— *The Mechanical Processes of the Historian.* (Helps to Students
of History.) S.P.C.K.
> Full of useful hints for anyone writing a thesis or printing it.

Phillimore, W. P. W. *How to write the History of a Family.* 1887;
supplement 1896.

Piggott, Sir Francis. 'Practical Notes on Historical Research.'
Trans. of the Royal Hist. Soc., 4th ser., vol. v (1922).

Rye, Walter. *Records and Record Searching.* London, 1897.

Stamp, A. E. 'The Historical Student and the Public Record
Office. A Retrospect.' *Trans. of the Royal Hist. Soc.,*
4th ser., vol. xl (1928).
> A vivid account of the changes of the last forty years.

Willard, J. F., Morris, W. A. and others. *The English Government at Work, 1327–1336.* 3 vols. 1940–50.

Woodward, E. L. *War and Peace in Europe, 1815–1870, and other
essays.* London, 1931.
> Valuable for nineteenth-century material and its use.

CHANCERY

Ayloffe, Joseph. *Calendars of the Ancient Charters etc. and of the
Welsh and Scottish Rolls, now remaining in the Tower of London.*
London, 1774.

Baldwin, James F. 'The Chancery of the Duchy of Lancaster.' *Bulletin of the Inst. of Hist. Research*, vol. iv, no. 12 (1927).

Bémont, C. *Rôles gascons*. Supplément, T. 1, Introduction. 1896. (*Documents inédits*.)

—— 'Un *Rotulus Finium* retrouvé, 1242–3.' *Bulletin philologique et historique*, 1924.

Calendar of Patent Rolls, Edw. III. Preface to vol. i. London, 1891.

Crump, C. G. 'Eo quod expressa mentio', &c., in *Essays presented to R. L. Poole*. Oxford, 1927.

Davis, H. W. C. *Regesta Regum Anglo-Normannorum*, vol. i, Oxford, 1913.

> The Introduction contains a good summary of the OE. and Norman Chancery to 1100.

Delisle, Léopold. *Recueil des Actes de Henri II*. Introduction. 1909.

> The best account of the Anglo-Norman Chancery in the twelfth century.

Dibben, Lila. 'Chancellor and Keeper of the Seal under Henry III.' *E.H.R.* xxvii. 39–51.

Hardy, T. D. *Catalogue of Lord Chancellors, Keepers of the Great Seal, Masters of the Rolls*, &c. 1843.

—— *Rotuli Litterarum Patentium*. Fol. Introduction. 1833.
Reprinted 1835 as *Description of the Patent Rolls*.

—— *Rotuli Litterarum Clausarum*. 2 vols. Fol. Introduction. 1833, 1844.

—— *Rotuli Chartarum 1199–1216*. Fol. Introduction. 1837.

Johnson, C. *Calendar of Liberate Rolls*. Vol. i. Introduction. 1917.

*Lyte, Sir Henry Maxwell. *Historical Notes on the Great Seal*. H.M. Stationery Office, 1926.

> The definitive work on the actual operations of the English Chancery.

Pollard, A. F. 'Wolsey and the Great Seal.' *Bulletin of the Inst. of Hist. Research*, vol. vii, no. 20 (1929).

Report of Lords Commissioners on the Court of Chancery. 1740.

Sanders, G. W. *Orders of the High Court of Chancery*. London, 1845.

Stamp, A. E. 'Some Notes on the Court and Chancery of Henry III' in *Essays presented to James Tait*. Manchester, 1933.

Tout, T. F. 'The Household of the Chancery and its Disintegration' in *Essays presented to R. L. Poole*. Oxford, 1927.

Willard, James F. 'The dating and delivery of letters patent and writs in the fourteenth century.' *Bulletin of the Inst. of Hist. Research*, vol. x, no. 28 (1932).

Wilkinson, Bertie. *The Chancery under Edward III*. Manchester Univ. Press, 1929.

EXCHEQUER

Crump, C. G., and Johnson, Charles. 'Tables of Bullion coined under Edward I, II, and III.' *Numismatic Chronicle*, 4th ser., vol. xiii.

Davies, J. C. *Baronial Opposition to Edward II*.
    Valuable for material culled from the Memoranda Rolls.

Devon, Frederick. *Issue Roll of Thomas de Brantingham*. London, 1835.
    The Issue Roll of 44 Edward III translated into English.
—— *Issues of the Exchequer*. London, 1837.
    Extracts from the Issue Rolls. Translated. Very useful.

Encyclopaedia Britannica, art. 'Exchequer'.

Fanshawe, Sir Thomas. *The Practice of the Exchequer Court*. London, 1658.

Galbraith, V. H. 'The Tower as an Exchequer Record Office in the reign of Edward II.' *Essays presented to T. F. Tout*. 1925.

George, Mrs. Eric. 'Notes on the Origin of the Declared Account', in *E.H.R.* xxxi. 41–58.

Gras, N. S. B. *The early English Customs System*. Harvard, 1918.

Hall, Hubert. *Introduction to the Study of the Pipe Rolls*. Pipe Roll Soc., no. 3. 1884.
—— *Red Book of the Exchequer*. 3 vols. Rolls Series, 1896.
—— *The Antiquities and Curiosities of the Exchequer*. London, 1898.
—— *Receipt Roll of the Exchequer for Michaelmas Term 31 Henry II* (1185). Fol. London, 1899.

Jenkinson, H. 'The Records of Exchequer Receipts from the English Jewry.' *Trans. of the Jewish Hist. Soc. of England*, viii. 19 sqq.
—— 'Exchequer Tallies', in *Archaeologia*, lxii, 367 sqq.

*Johnson, Charles. *Pipe Roll Society*: New Series. Vol. i. *2 Richard II*. Introduction. 1925.

  A simple description of the early Pipe Rolls.

—— **Dialogus de Scaccario*. Nelson's Med. Classics, 1950.

Johnstone, Hilda. 'The Queen's Exchequer under the three Edwards', in *Essays presented to James Tait*. Manchester, 1933.

*Madox, Thomas. *The History and Antiquities of the Exchequer*. Fol. 1711. Quarto ed. 2 vols. 1769.

  Not yet superseded.

Mills, Mabel H. 'Experiments in Exchequer Procedure 1200–1232.' *Trans. of the Royal Hist. Soc.*, 4th ser., vol. viii (1925).

—— 'The Reforms at the Exchequer.' *Trans. of the Royal Hist. Soc.*, 4th ser., vol. x (1927).

*—— *The Pipe Roll for 1295*. Surrey Membrane. *Surrey Record Society*, no. xxi (1924).

  Indispensable for the study of the Pipe Rolls in the thirteenth century or later.

Mitchell, S. K. *Taxation in Medieval England*, edited S. Painter. Yale Univ. Press, 1951.

Newton, A. P. 'The Treasurer of the Chamber under the early Tudors.' *E.H.R.* xxxii. 348 sqq.

—— 'The Establishment of the Great Farm of the English Customs.' *Trans. of the Royal Hist. Soc.*, 4th ser., vol. i (1918).

Palgrave, Sir Francis. *Antient Kalendars and Inventories of the Exchequer*. London, 1836.

Poole, R. L. *The Exchequer in the Twelfth Century*. Oxford, 1912.

Power, Eileen, and Postan, M. M. 'Tables of Enrolled Customs and Subsidy Accounts (1399–1482).' *Studies in English Trade in the Fifteenth Century*. 1933.

Ramsay, Sir J. H. 'The Origin of the name "Pipe Roll".' *E.H.R.* xxvi (1911).

Richardson, H. G. 'The Exchequer Year.' *Trans. of the Royal Hist. Soc.*, 4th ser., no. 8 (1925). With a supplementary note in the next volume.

Steel, Anthony. 'The Practice of Assignment in the Later Fourteenth Century.' *E.H.R.* xliii (1928).

—— 'The marginalia of the Treasurer's Receipt Rolls.' *Bulletin of the Inst. of Hist. Research*, vol. vii, no. 20 (1929), and vol. viii, no. 22 (1930).

Turner, G. J. 'The Sheriff's Farm.' *Trans. of the Royal Hist. Soc.*, vol. xii (1898).

Willard, James F. 'A brief guide to the records dealing with the taxes upon movables.' *Bulletin of the Inst. of Hist. Research*, vol. iii, no. 7 (1925).

—— 'Taxation Boroughs and Parliamentary Boroughs', in *Essays presented to James Tait*. Manchester, 1933.

—— 'The Memoranda Rolls and the Remembrancers', in *Essays presented to T. F. Tout*. Manchester, 1925.

—— *Parliamentary Taxes on Personal Property, 1290–1334*. Cambridge, Mass., 1934.

COURTS OF LAW

Bolland, W. C. *Eyre of Kent*. Selden Soc., 1910–13.

—— *The General Eyre*. Cambridge, 1922.

Cam, Helen M. 'On the Material available in the Eyre Rolls.' *Bulletin of the Inst. of Hist. Research*, vol. iii, no. 9 (1926).

——* *The Hundred and the Hundred Rolls*. London, 1930.

Dugdale, W. *Origines Juridiciales*. 1671.

Fitzherbert, A. *La Novelle Natura Brevium*. London, 1534.

Foster, Canon C. W. *Feet of Fines for Lincoln*. Lincoln Record Soc. (17). Horncastle, 1920.

Fowler, R. C. 'Legal Proofs of Age.' *E.H.R.* xxii (1907).

Hastings, Margaret. *The Court of Common Pleas in the XV century*. New York, 1947.

Legal and Manorial Formularies in memory of J. P. Gilson. Oxford, 1933.

Maitland, F. W. 'The History of the Register of Original Writs.' *Collected Papers*, vol. ii.

—— *Pleas of the Crown for the County of Gloucester*. London, 1884.

Phillimore, W. P. W. *Coram Rege Roll, Trinity Term, 25 Edw. I. 1297*. British Record Soc. (19). London, 1898.

Plucknett, T. F. T. *History of the Common Law*. 4th ed., 1948.

Registrum Omnium Brevium. London, 1531.

Report of Lords Commissioners on Courts of Justice. 1816.

Richardson, H. G. 'Year Books and Plea Rolls as Sources of

Historical Information.' *Trans. of the Royal Hist. Soc.*, 4th ser., vol. v (1922).

Sayles, G. O. *Select Cases in the Court of King's Bench under Edward I.* 3 vols. 1936–9. Selden Society.

Stenton, Doris M. *The Earliest Northamptonshire Assize Rolls, A.D. 1202 and 1203.* Northamptonshire Record Soc. (5). Lincoln and London, 1930.

—— *The Earliest Lincolnshire Assize Rolls,* A.D. *1202–1209.* Lincoln Record Soc. (22). 1926.

Turner, G. J. *Feet of Fines for the County of Huntingdon.* Introduction. Cambridge, 1913.

Winfield, P. H. *The Chief Sources of English Legal History.* Cambridge, 1925.

PARLIAMENT AND COUNCIL

Baldwin, James F. *The King's Council.* Oxford, 1913.

Edwards, J. G. 'The Parliamentary Committee of 1398.' *E.H.R.* xl (1925).

—— 'The Personnel of the Commons in Parliament under Edward I and Edward II.' *Essays presented to T. F. Tout.* Manchester, 1925.

Interim Report of the Committee on the House of Commons Personnel and Politics 1264–1832. H.M. Stationery Office, 1932.

Lewis, N. B. 'The "Continual Council" in the Early Years of Richard II, 1377–80.' *E.H.R.* xli (1926).

—— 'Re-election to Parliament in the reign of Richard II.' *E.H.R.* xlviii (1933).

McFarlane, K. B. 'Parliament and Bastard Feudalism.' *Trans. of the Royal Hist. Soc.*, 1944.

*Maitland, F. W. *Memoranda de Parliamento de 1305.* Introduction. Rolls Series, 1893.

Palgrave, Sir Francis. *Parliamentary Writs.* 2 vols. Record Commission. 1827–34.

—— *An essay upon the original authority of the King's council.* Record Commission. London, 1834.

Pares, Richard. *Colonial Blockade and Neutral Rights, 1739–63.* Oxford, 1938.

Parliaments and Councils 1066–1688. 1839.

Pollard, A. F. *The Evolution of Parliament.* 2nd ed. 1926.

Pugh, R. B. 'The Patent Rolls of the Interregnum.' *Bulletin of the Inst. of Hist. Research*, vol. xxiii, no. 68.

Richardson, H. G., and Sayles, G. 'The Early Records of the English Parliaments.' *Bulletin of the Inst. of Hist. Research*, vol. v, no. 15 (1928), and vol. vi, no. 17 (1928) and no. 18 (1929).

———— 'The Parliaments of Edward III.' *Bulletin of the Inst. of Hist. Research*, vol. viii, no. 23 (1930), and ix, no. 25 (1931).

Roskell, J. S. 'The medieval speakers for the Commons in Parliament.' *Bulletin of the Inst. of Hist. Research*, vol. xxiii, no. 67.

—— 'The social composition of the Commons in a fifteenth-century parliament.' *Bulletin of the Inst. of Hist. Research*, vol. xxiv, no. 70.

Smith, J. H. *Appeals to the Privy Council from American Plantations.* New York, 1950.

HOUSEHOLD

Johnson, Charles. 'The Keeper of Papal Bulls', in *Essays presented to T. F. Tout.* Manchester, 1925.

—— 'The System of Account in the Wardrobe of Edward I.' *Trans. of the Royal Hist. Soc.*, 4th ser., vol. vi, pp. 50–72.

Johnson, J. H. 'The Wardrobe under Edward II.' *Trans. of the Royal Hist. Soc.*, 4th ser., vol. xii, pp. 75–104.

Johnstone, Hilda. 'The Wardrobe and Household of Henry son of Edward I.' *Bulletin of the John Ryland Library*, vol. vii, no. 3 (1923).

Liber Quotidianus Garderobae. 28 Edward I. Soc. of Antiquaries. London, 1787.

Mirot, Léon, and Deprez, E. 'Les Ambassades anglaises pendant la Guerre de Cent Ans (1327–1450).' *Bibliothèque de l'École des Chartes*, 1898–1900.

Ordinances for the Royal Household from Edward III to William and Mary. Society of Antiquaries. London, 1790.

STATE PAPERS

Evans, F. M. P. *The Principal Secretary of State.* Manchester Univ. Press, 1923.

Lomas, Mrs. S. C. 'The State Papers of the Early Stuarts and the Interregnum.' *Trans. of the Royal Hist. Soc.* New Series, vol. xvi (1902).

Otway-Ruthven, A. J. *The King's Secretary and the Signet Office in the XV century.* Cambridge, 1937.

State Paper Office. *Introduction to the Calendar of Documents relating to the History of*: in *D. K. Report*, xxx, App., pp. 212 sqq.

Thomson, M. A. *The Secretaries of State, 1681–1782.* Oxford, 1932.

FORESTS

Bazeley, Margaret L. 'The Extent of the English Forest in the Thirteenth Century.' *Trans. of the Royal Hist. Soc.*, 4th ser., vol. iv (1921).

Turner, G. J. *Select Pleas of the Forest.* Selden Soc. (13). London, 1901.

CHRONOLOGY

Bond, John J. *Handy Book of Rules and Tables for verifying Dates.* London, 1889.

*Cheney, C. R. *Handbook of Dates.* Royal Hist. Soc., 1945.

Fry, E. A. *Almanacks for students of English History, being a set of 35 Almanacks arranged for every day upon which Easter can fall.* London, 1915.

Nicholas, Sir Harris. *Notitia Historica.* London, 1824.

—— *Chronology of History.* London, 1840.

*Poole, R. L. *Medieval Reckonings of Times.* (Helps to Students of History.) S.P.C.K., 1918.

—— 'The Beginning of the Year in the Middle Ages.' *Proceedings of the British Academy*, vol. x.

—— *Studies in Chronology and History*, edited A. L. Poole. Oxford, 1934.

Powicke, F. M., and Cheney, C. R. *Handbook of British Chronology.* Royal Hist. Soc., 1939.

*Stamp, A. E. *Methods of Chronology.* Historical Association, 1933.

Wallis, J. E. W. *English Regnal Years and Titles.* (Helps to Students of History.) S.P.C.K., 1921.

PALAEOGRAPHY, ETC.

*Baxter, J. H. and Johnson, C. *Medieval Latin Word List.* Oxford, 1934.

Cheney, C. R. *English Bishops' Chanceries.* Manchester University Press, 1950.

Du Cange, C. Dufresne. *Glossarium mediae et infimae Latinitatis.* 7 vols. Paris, 1840–50.

*Jenkinson, Hilary. *The Later Court Hands in England.* Cambridge University Press, 1927.

—— 'Elizabethan Handwritings.' *Trans. of the Bibliographical Soc. (The Library),* 1922.

—— 'The Use of Arabic and Roman Numerals in English Archives.' *Journal of the Society of Antiquaries,* July, 1926.

*Johnson, Charles, and Jenkinson, Hilary. *English Court Hand.* Clarendon Press, 1915.

Lyte, Sir H. C. Maxwell. ' "U" and "V". A note on Palaeography.' *Bulletin of the Inst. of Hist. Research,* vol. ii, no. 6 (1925).

Maitland, F. W. *Introduction to 'Year Books, 1 and 2 Edward II'.* Selden Society (17). London, 1903.
    Useful for the French of the Year Books.

*Martin, Charles Trice. *The Record Interpreter.* London, 1910. Contains a good working vocabulary of Latin words found in the Records.

Thompson, Sir E. M. *Handbook of Greek and Latin Palaeography.* London, 1906.
    The last section is on 'Court Hand'.

SEALS

Birch, Walter de Gray. *Catalogue of Seals in the British Museum.* London, 1887–1900.

Blair, C. Hunter. *Seals of Northumberland and Durham.* Kendal, 1923, 1924.

Greenwell, Rev. W., and Blair, C. Hunter. *Durham Seals.* Newcastle, 1914, 1915.

—— —— *Catalogue of the Ecclesiastical Seals in the Treasury of the Dean and Chapter of Durham.* Newcastle, 1917–19.

Jenkinson, Hilary. 'A Seal of Edward II for Scottish Affairs.' *Antiquaries Journal,* vol. xi (1931).

Kingsford, H. S. *Seals.* (Helps to Students of History.) **S.P.C.K.**

Laboree, L. W., and Moody, Robert E. 'The Seal of the Privy Council.' *E.H.R.* xliii (1928).

Salter, H. 'The Half Seal.' *Bulletin of the Inst. of Hist. Research,* vol. x. no. 30 (1933).

Wilkinson, Bertie. 'The Seals of the two Benches under Edward III.' *E.H.R.* xlii (1927).

Wyon, A. B., and Wyon, Allan. *Great Seals of England.* London, 1887.

See also p. 92, Maxwell Lyte, *Historical Notes on the Great Seal.*

MISCELLANEOUS

Andrews, C. M. *Guide to the Materials for American History in the Public Record Office, London.* Washington, D.C. 2 vols. 1912, 1914.

Aspinall, A. *Early English Trade Unions.* 1949.
Useful as a guide to Home Office Papers of the early 19th century.

Cam, Helen. *Liberties and Communities in Medieval England.* Cambridge University Press, 1944.

Clark, G. N. *Guide to English Commercial Statistics.* 1938.

Coate, Mary. 'The Duchy of Cornwall: its history and administration.' *Trans. of the Royal Hist. Soc.* 4th ser., vol. x (1927).

Crompton, J. R. 'Some documents in the P.R.O. relating to early Public Health administration.' *Bulletin of the Inst. of Hist. Research,* vol. v. no. 14 (1927).

Galbraith, V. H. *Studies in the Public Records.* Nelson, 1948.

Gilson, J. P. *Students' Guide to the MSS. of the British Museum.* (Helps to Students of History.) S.P.C.K.

Higham, C. S. *The Colonial Entry Books.* (Helps to Students of History.) S.P.C.K., 1921.

Hoyt, R. S. *The Royal Demesne 1066–1272.* Ithaca, New York, 1950.

Hurstfield, J. 'Lord Burghley as Master of the Court of Wards.' *Trans. of the Royal Hist. Soc.,* vol. xxxi (1949).

Knoop, D., and Jones, G. P. *The Medieval Mason.* Manchester Univ. Press, 1933.
Essential for the study of building accounts.

Lapsley, G. *Palatinate of Durham.* Harvard Historical Studies.

Perroy, E. *Diplomatic Correspondence of Richard II.* Camden Soc., 1933.
    A valuable introduction on the 'small seals'.
Roscoe, E. S. *History of the English Prize Court.* London, 1924.
Ruddock, A. A. 'The Earliest Records of the High Court of Admiralty.' *Bulletin of the Inst. of Hist. Research*, vol. xxii, no. 66.
Somerville, R. 'Duchy of Lancaster Records.' *Trans. of the Royal Hist. Soc.*, 1947.
Story, J. *Notes on the principles and practice of prize courts.* London, 1854.

APPENDIX II

Rules and Regulations made by the Master of the Rolls respecting the Public Use of the Records[1]

Hours and conditions of attendance

1. The Search Rooms shall be open to persons desiring to inspect Records or Documents on every day, except Sunday, Good Friday, Saturday before Easter, Easter Monday, Saturday before Whit Sunday, Whit Monday, August Bank Holiday, Christmas Day, Boxing Day, and any other days which may be appointed for Public or Privilege Holidays.

The hours of admission and attendance shall be, for Literary Searches from 10.0 to 5.30, except on Saturdays, when they shall be from 10.0 to 2.0; and, for Searches subject to the payment of fees, from 10.0 to 4.30, except on Saturdays, when they shall be from 10.0 to 1.0.

2. All persons making use of the Search Rooms for the purpose of consulting the Records or the Indexes thereto shall write their names and full addresses, daily, in the Attendance Book kept for the purpose.

---

[1] Reprinted from the official regulations by permission of the Controller of H.M. Stationery Office.

3. No umbrellas or sticks shall be taken into any Search Room.

Records open to inspection

4. Records in the statutory custody of the Master of the Rolls, Records of the Duchy of Lancaster, and Records of the late State Paper Office, shall be open to public inspection subject to the conditions mentioned below and to the payment of the Fees specified in the Schedule hereto.

5. Any Person wishing to inspect such Records of an earlier date than the year 1843 free of charge shall make a written application for a Student's Ticket to the Secretary of the Public Record Office on the form provided for that purpose: a person of alien status shall, in addition, ask his Embassy or Legation to apply to the Foreign Office for a Letter of Introduction on his behalf.

6. Records of Departments of State deposited in the Public Record Office shall be open to inspection, by persons holding Student's Tickets, down to the years specified by the Heads of such Departments.

7. Records deposited in the Public Record Office by Departments of State, but not opened to public inspection, shall only be produced subject to such conditions as the Heads of the respective Departments shall from time to time prescribe.

8. A General Catalogue of Lists, Indexes, Calendars, &c., intended for the use of the Public is kept in the Search Rooms: Lists, Indexes, &c., not mentioned in this Catalogue shall not be produced without permission of the Officer in charge of the Search Rooms.

9. Records not mentioned in the Search Room Lists, and Records in course of arrangement, shall not be produced without permission of the Officer in charge of the Search Rooms.

10. Documents which are of exceptional value, or are

unwieldy, unstamped or fragile, shall be examined under such conditions as the Officer in charge of the Room shall, in the particular case, think requisite for their safety: no person shall be entitled to examine Documents which have been labelled 'Unfit for Production'.

Issue and return of records

11. A separate ticket shall be clearly written and signed by every person desiring to inspect any Document for each Document required; and this ticket shall be given by such person to the Officer in charge of the Room before any Document is produced to the applicant.

12. No person shall have more than three Documents inclusive out at one time except by special permission of the Officer in charge of the Room.

13. Immediately after the conclusion of a search Documents shall be returned by the person to whom they have been produced to the Officer in charge of the Room, or to one of the Attendants, in exchange for the tickets referring to them; and all such persons shall be held responsible for the Documents issued to them so long as their tickets shall remain with an Official of the Public Record Office.

14. Persons wishing to retain Documents for use after the first day of production shall fill in and sign the portion of the Ticket of Application which is marked 'kept out' before leaving on that day; and shall apply for each Document, when it is next required, on the ticket specially provided for the purpose.

Handling and treatment of records

15. The introduction of bags or parcels into the Search Rooms is not normally forbidden; but they shall not be placed upon the Tables.

16. No person shall lean upon, crumple, or touch with a pencil point or wetted finger any Documents or Books

belonging to the Public Record Office, or place upon them the paper on which he or she is writing; and Documents made up in volumes or files shall, whenever possible, be placed upon the rests provided for the purpose.

17. No person other than an Officer of the Public Record Office shall make any mark upon, or any alteration in the writing of, any Document or Book belonging to that Office.

18. Liquid Ink shall not be used.

19. Tracings of Documents shall not be made by any person without specific permission from the Officer in charge of the Room.

20. Documents, Books, or other articles belonging to the Public Record Office shall not be removed from one room to another without the specific permission of the Officer in charge of the Room; nor by any person other than an official.

21. Works of Reference taken from the open shelves of the Search Rooms shall be returned to their correct places immediately after use.

Photography

22. Reproduction of Documents by a number of photographic processes is undertaken officially by the Department; and detailed information with regard to this service is given in a separate leaflet, which may be obtained in the Search Rooms or by postal application to the Secretary. As the studio accommodation at the disposal of the Department is very limited, outside photographers can only in exceptional circumstances, and on special conditions, be permitted to work in the Office.

23. Photographs of Public Records shall not be reproduced except by permission of the Department. Applicants for such permission shall specify the context in which the reproduction will appear; and it shall be

understood to extend only to reproduction in that context. To ensure accuracy of reference, any caption or description which it is proposed to attach to such a reproduction shall be submitted for approval by the Department.

General rules

24. Silence must be maintained in the Search Rooms and adjacent passages so far as possible.

25. All suggestions or complaints in regard to the administration of the Search Rooms shall be made in the first instance to the Officer in charge of the Room concerned.

26. The Officer in charge of any Search Room shall be empowered to exclude persons from the Public Record Office for any of the following reasons: wilful breach of any of the foregoing Rules and Regulations; persistent disregard of the Officer's authority; damage of any sort to any Document or article belonging to the Public Record Office; and conduct, language, habits, unseemly dress, or any other matter offensive, or likely to be reasonably offensive, to others using the Public Record Office: provided always that the exclusion of any person shall be forthwith notified in writing, with the cause thereof, to the Deputy Keeper; who shall enquire into the circumstances, and whose order, unless reversed by the Master of the Rolls, shall be final.

Short Title, &c.

27. These Rules may be cited as the Public Use of the Records Rules, 1949 [*Statutory Instruments*, 1949, *No.* 2211]; and shall come into operation on the 1st day of January, 1950, in substitution for the existing Rules and Regulations, which shall as from that day cease to have any effect.

17 *November* 1949.

(*Signed*)   RAYMOND EVERSHED, M.R.

SCHEDULE

TABLE OF FEES

	£	s.	d.
For the inspection of any Document, *per diem*	0	1	6
For the inspection of a number of Documents, not exceeding ten, in any one suit, action or matter, *per diem*	0	4	0
For Certified Manuscript Copies:			
for a copy not exceeding five folios of 72 words	0	15	0
for longer copies, *per folio*	0	3	0

[Copies for certification are normally made by the 'Photostat' process, the charges for which are given in the leaflet mentioned in paragraph 22 above: but Manuscript Copies of Documents in Latin or French, or in ancient handwritings, may be supplied on request.]

	£	s.	d.
For certifying 'Photostat' or other Photographic Copies, *per sheet*	0	1	0
For making by tracing or for colouring Copies of Maps, Plans, Drawings, &c., *per hour*	0	4	0
For attendance at the Royal Courts of Justice or elsewhere to produce Records for the purpose of evidence, *per diem*	3	3	0
For attendance on the Master of the Rolls on a *Vacatur*	0	10	0
For vacating, pursuant to the Clerical Disabilities Act, 1870, (Amendment) Measure, 1934, Enrolment of a Deed of Relinquishment of Holy Orders	0	5	0

APPENDIX III

Regulations in force as to the conditions under which Departmental Records are open to inspection

(1) ADMIRALTY.
(i) All *Logs* and *Journals*, *Muster Books* and *Pay Lists* of Ships are open without restriction as to date.
(ii) Other records are open to 1902.

(2) MINISTRY OF AGRICULTURE AND FISHERIES.
(i) The *Deeds and Evidences*, and those *Manorial Documents* which are earlier than 1886 are open without restriction.
(ii) Other records are open on payment of fees.

(3) LORD CHAMBERLAIN'S OFFICE.
   Open to 1885.

(4) CHARITY COMMISSION.
   Such records as have been transmitted are open without restriction.

(5) COLONIAL OFFICE.
   (i) Records of the *West Indies Encumbered Estates Commission*, and all volumes of printed *Gazettes, Minutes of Legislative Councils, Journals of Houses of Assembly, Colonial Sessional Papers* and similar documents which may be presumed to have been made public in the Colonies, are open without restriction.
   (ii) Other records are open to 1902, with the exception of the *Irish Crimes Records.*

(6) COMMONWEALTH RELATIONS OFFICE.
   All printed documents which may be presumed to have been made public, are open without restriction.
   Other records are not open.

(7) BOARD OF CUSTOMS AND EXCISE.
   Such records as have been transmitted are open without restriction.

(8) BOARD OF EDUCATION.
   Such records as have been transmitted are open without restriction.

(9) EXCHEQUER AND AUDIT OFFICE.
   Open to 1850.

(10) FOREIGN OFFICE.
   (i) *Ink Stamps* and *Seals* are open without restriction.
   (ii) *Acts of the Peace Conference*, Parts 1 to 7, are open.
   (iii) Other records are open to 1902.

(11) MINISTRY OF HEALTH.
   With the exception of *War of 1914–18, War Refugees Committee* the records are open without restriction.

(12) HOME OFFICE.
   Open to 1878.
   Exceptions: (i) The *Census Papers, Population Returns* are only open on payment of fees.

    (ii) The records of the Prison Commission, with the exception of the *Sessions Papers, Old Bailey*, are not open.

    (iii) Records relating to *Caroline, Princess of Wales* are not open to inspection without special permit.

(13) INDIA OFFICE.

The *Commissions* are open without restriction. No other records have as yet been transmitted.

(14) BOARD OF INLAND REVENUE.

    (i) *Apprenticeship Books* and *Deeds and Evidences* are open without restriction.

    (ii) Other records are not open.

(15) LAND REVENUE RECORD OFFICE.

Open to 1831. Records dated 1832 and later are not open without special permit and the payment of fees.

(16) LAW OFFICERS' DEPARTMENT.

Open without restriction.

(17) NATIONAL DEBT OFFICE.

Open to 1902.

(18) PAYMASTER GENERAL'S OFFICE.

Open to 1878.

(19) PRIVY COUNCIL OFFICE.

Open to 1902.

(20) PRIVY PURSE OFFICE.

Visitors' Books are open to inspection in the Legal Search Room.

Other records are not open.

(21) PUBLIC RECORD OFFICE.

    (i) *Transcripts* and *Manorial Records Deposited* are open without restriction.

    (ii) *Gifts* are usually open to the same date as the Departmental Records to which they relate.

    (iii) Other records are not open.

(22) SIGNET OFFICE.

Open to 1878.

(23) MINISTRY OF SUPPLY.

Open to 1902.

(24) LORD STEWARD'S OFFICE.
   Open to 1885.

(25) BOARD OF TRADE.
   Open to 1885.

(26) MINISTRY OF TRANSPORT.
   Open to 1902.

(27) TREASURY.
   Open to 1902.

(28) TREASURY SOLICITOR.
   Records of the *West New Jersey Society* are open, with certain
      exceptions, after 1821.
   Other records are not open.

(29) WAR OFFICE.
   (i) All *Pay Lists, Muster Rolls* and *Monthly Returns* of Regi-
         ments are open without restriction.
   (ii) Records of the *Judge Advocate General* are open to 1865.
   (iii) *South African War Claims* are open to 1905; and the other
         records are open to 1902.

(30) MINISTRY OF WORKS.
   Open without restriction.

Records of the following departments are not open to public
inspection without special permit:

   ASSISTANCE BOARD.

   CIVIL SERVICE COMMISSION.

   CHURCH COMMISSION.

   FORESTRY COMMISSION.

   MINISTRY OF MUNITIONS.

   MINISTRY OF NATIONAL SERVICE.

   REGISTRAR GENERAL.

   OFFICE OF WOODS, FORESTS AND LAND REVENUES.

   NATIONAL INSURANCE AUDIT DEPARTMENT.

INDEX